Afrikan People and European Holidays: A Mental Genocide

BOOK TWO

Ishakamusa Barashango

AFRIKAN WORLD BOOKS
2217 Pennsylvania Ave., Baltimore, MD 21217
410-383-2006
www.afrikanworldbooks.com

•

October 2001

First Printing **February 1983**

Cover: Mary Esther Greer

DEDICATION

This book is dedicated to Brother Ahmed Evans, one of the unsung heroes of the Black rebellions of the decade of the Sixties and the early Seventies, who really knew the meaning of the phrase "Give me liberty or give me death." For he counted the liberty and true freedom of his people dearer than his own personal well-being. This warrior was captured and held in the Ohio State Concentration Camp on death row until the day of his untimely passing, through what is reported to have been caused by cancer. To those lovers of liberty all over the world this brother will never be forgotten. In the words of the Last Poets, "Blessed are those who struggle, oppression is worse than the grave, better to die for a noble cause than to live and die a slave."

This book is also dedicated to Brother Irving Davis, a son of Afrika who dearly loved his Mother and all her children wherever they were scattered over the world. And he demonstrated this love by working untiringly to raise funds to aid Afrikan Liberation struggles around the globe, especially those being waged on the Afrikan continent, as well as his work and leadership in the Black reparations efforts for Afrikan People here in the United States. I personally have had the pleasure of debating with this brilliant mind on several occasions and the memory and fortitude of this truly beautiful Afrikan man will live on in my psyche forever. The physical remains of Brother Irving Davis have been deposited in his homeland at the base of the Great Pyramid during services conducted by High Priest Dr. Yosef ben Jochannon. Live on great spirit, live on in the wind. Live on great spirit, stir your people onward to their true freedom.

FOREWORD

Originally we had intended to include the section entitled "Easter, the Festival of Fools" in this book. Due to the limitation of time and resources, as well as the attention given to the narrative outline of the British Empire and its direct relationship to America's Independence Day: The Fourth of You-Lie, it became expedient for us to confine the contents of Book II within the context of this subject.

During the course of the writers' research and collection of data a voluminous amount of material was compiled. Therefore the greatest task set before us was to decided what to include and what to leave out of this offering. This arbitration was sometimes agonizing to say the lest. Nevertheless, we sincerely believe the end product will prove to be of great value to the reader.

Much of the information which, out of necessity, was set aside has been reserved for use as supplementary material to the heading American Independence Day: The Fourth of You-Lie along with "Easter, the Festival of Fools" and other pertinent subject matter in *Afrikan People and European Holidays: A Mental Genocide*, Book III.

Thank you for your interest and patience in this matter.

The Publishers

TABLE OF CONTENTS

Dr. Ishakamusa Barashango
April 27, 1938 - January 14, 2004

AFRIKAN WORLD BOOKS
2217 Pennsylvania Ave., Baltimore, MD 21217
410-383-2006
www.afrikanworldbooks.com

Chapter One

America's Independence Day:
The Fourth of You-Lie

CHAPTER ONE

AMERICA'S INDEPENDENCE DAY:
THE FOURTH OF YOU-LIE

July 4th is the date annually set aside to commemorate the gathering of 54 "land grabbing theives" who were convened at the Second Continental Congress to determine their own destiny as white men (Euro-Americans) in a British dominated colonial sphere which at this time in world history, according to Brother Malcolm, it was said that "the sun never set on the British Empire". In order to comprehend the true meaning of this event from an Afrikan worldview perspective Black People must clearly understand that America's strike for independence from the British colonial empire, for all of its lofty proclamations of a "liberty and justice for all" was in no way inclusive of theBlack population residing here in the thirteen colonies.

Most Black People in colonial America were in bondage to white plantation owners and merchants. The only time that the Black Man was taken into account during this principal epoch of Euro-American history was when the slave masters stumbled on the idea that we could be used as their shields against British muskets, therefore minimizing for whites the risk of being mortally wounded. Thus many slaveowners sent their Black bondsmen to the front lines to serve as targets and cannon fodder for the protection of the not so patriotic colonial Americans.

The war of the American Revolution was not commissioned with the objective of altering Black People's status here as "hewers of wood and drawers of water", except to add more weights to our already backbreaking burdens and plunge us deeper into slavery. That is why we refer to this day as the Fourth of You-Lie. The Euro-Americans blatantly lied to us when they promised us freedom if we would fight for their liberation from Britian and the tyranny of King George as they called it. This was one of the bitterest lies in the history of the world for the majority of Black People in the United States were far worse off at the close of the Revolutionary War than they were before it began, especially with the coming of the cotton gin in 1793 and the evolution of king cotton and its super role in the industrialization of the 18th Century.

Those eloquent lies about freedom, justice and liberty for all did not include Black Folks in the "all". Even at the time of the

1

framing of the United States Constitution Blacks were considered to be only three-fifths of a person. This same lying to and unfairness of treatment and disenfranchisement of the Black Man on the part of the whites continues even unto this day of the much talked about Reaganomics and before we as Afrikan people who reside here in the borders of the United States can set things right for ourselves we must clearly understand the nature of the people we were dealing with then and are forced to contend with now. That is the main purpose of this section, the Fourth-Of-You-Lie.

In order for us to get a full grasp and comprehensive meaning of this event we must stop here and take a panoramic view of a narrative outline of the history of the British Empire. As we proceed along this course we should ever bear in mind that the historical phenomenon of the formation of the United States and its Revolutionary War was merely an extension of Great Britian's attempt at world empire. America's secession from Britian was merely the act of a wayward daughter rising in rebellion against her mother, for America is England's child through the unholy union of colonial exploitation and the Afrikan slave trade and as we shall clearly see further on in our studies Britian was the step-daughter of the Roman Empire, which was the illegitimate daughter of the so-called Greek civilization, which in its turn was the foster child of the High Culture Civilizations of Ancient Ethiopia and Egypt. Also in our academic travels we shall further observe that during the long period of the Afrikan colonization of Greece and other city-states in Mediterranean Europe there was a renaissance of world order, technical and natural sciences and a high moral sense, the knowledge of right and wrong. This revival of civilization as generated by Afrikan colonists in that area occurred around 500 B.C.E.

Our cameo outline of the British Empire is in essence a case study of how most European nations generally developed and their resultant colonization of much of the 87% population peoples of color in the world. We are pursuing this line of study because it is important for us as a people to examine European history in its proper context. Just as it is absolutely essential that we study our own history, Afrikan History, then place the two side by side for comparative analysis. This methodology will present us with a clearer picture of the true facts which we as always should interpret from the perspective of an Afrikan World View.

The following sketches are not intended to be an exhaustive inquiry but rather an overview portrait of the British Empire. In these studies we will not attempt to enumerate all of the major events which took place in England or to chronogolize the profiles of all its monarchs. The main purpose of this outline is to touch on those episodes and personages that will provide us with a general background on the roots of British colonial expansion, the American Revolution and the Fourth of You-Lie. Proper treatment on the history of any nation even one with a sparse, ancient historical background such as that of caucasianized Britian cannot be adequately presented in a work of this nature. Nevertheless the following narratives will serve to bring a clearer understanding of this segment of the european saga and how it has and does affect the historical phenomenon of Afrikan People, this and other subjects on the origin of European nations will be dealt with in a forth coming work entitled *The History of Europe: An Afrikan World View.*

Through close observation we ascertain that most of the streets, towns, cities and states in the United States of America are named after English personalities and places. English is the official language of the United States and most of Canada and is widely used in Afrika and many other parts of the world. This is one of the results of the British Empire's wide-spread expansionism and exploitation of the overwhelming majority of peoples of color on the planet in general and the enslavement of the Afrikan in particular. Therefore, in order to efficiently study the history of any nation of people in the world whose dominant language is English, it becomes necessary to inquire into the evolutionary development of the British Empire. For example if we were to do an historical investigation of Nigeria of Ghana or any other Afrikan Nation where English is predominantly spoken we would need to study an outline of the British Empire.

In this study of the American Revolution and its attending events we are primarily concerned with the historical marvel of the 30-60 million English speaking population of the New Afrikan Nation here in America. In our learned quest we will closely follow the advice and example of Dr. Chancellor Williams, Dr. Frances Cress Welsing, Dr. Cheikh Anta Diop and other Black Scholars who have admonished us to know our natural enemy by studying and analyzing his culture and historical development; particularly as it relates to the Afrikan Experience.

The United Kingdom of Great Britian which includes Scotland, Wales and Northern Ireland is approximately the size of the state of oregon. England proper is about the size of the state of New York. It is interesting to note how this little island generally unsuitable for large populations within its own borders, once ruled much of the planet Earth. Just how this curious thing came to be is part of the subject matter covered in this narrative outline of the

British Empire.

Some may charge us as being one-sided in this particular account but what must be understood is that in this presentation we are showing the "other side of the coin". Previously Black People have generally been presented with a distorted view of world history, especially where we are concerned. Most textbooks written by European scholars have steadily reported the false notion that nothing of real value was happening in the world until they arrived. Hence the white man's "discovery mania". Nothing could be further from the truth. European historians, anthropologists, social scientists, etc. have caused many people in the whole world to view things from a "Pan-European" perspective. Now, in order to obtain a proper balance as we study this brief history of the development of the British Empire, it is imperative that we approach it from a New Afrikan World View. We do understand that some chroniclers will exaggerate from time to time for in the recording of events all people like to make themselves look good. But in the case of most European writers there is the tendency to cover up or play down their race's proverbial skeletons in the closet. In fact most of them recorded outright prefabricated lies. In this presentation we are endeavoring to help reverse that trend. Although many of the facts in this work are not generally known or reported in the context of an Afrikan World View they have nevertheless been well documented by thorough research.

As the facts are laid out for you in this study some may accuse me, as they did Joel A. Rogers, of trying to make everything and everybody of value in antiquity Afrikan. In a very real sense this is a historical fact recorded in monuments of stone all over the world. For in the early days of earth's history the Black Man dominated the globe. We will approach this subject with some detail in the following chapter. To many who have been well conditioned by europeanized thinking this may come as somewhat of a shock and may cause some to outright reject it. So if, perchance, you find yourself becoming adverse to the acceptance of a Black Scholars view we suggest you check out some European writers on this subject, such as Sir Godfrey Higgins who in his work *Anacalypsis*, Volume I, page 286 writes, "we have found the black complexion or something relating to it whenever we approach to the origins of nations." In another statement of that same Volume on page 10 Higgins, in seeming frustration, says that "whenever he went to study the origin of anything he always ended up at something black." At one period during the Black Man's domination of the world H.G. Wells in *A Short History of the World* records the state of most of the white race thusly, "Away in the forests of Europe were the blond nordic people - hunters and herdsmen. A lowly race, the primative civilizations saw very little of this race before 1,500 B.C." Similiar statements concerning the dominance and high culture of the Black Race and the lowly estate of Europeans on the earth at that time have been made by such European writers as Strabo, Herodotus, Gerald Massey and many others whom we shall encounter in our ensuing studies.

Although many historians claim to be objective very few, if any, of them ever are, all humans are subjected by something and that somehing is usually blood kinship and cultural identity. As a result of white academia's abstractions and supposed objectivity Black People have been made to see the world and it's history through another's eyes and this has been going on for such a long period of time and it makes it difficult for us to even begin to imagine our true place on the planet Earth. That is why those of us who are committed to the upliftment of the race advance the idea that we must view all things through our own eyes and experience, that is an Afrikan World View. Brother Haki Hadhubuti on the record *Rise Vision Comin* in reference to the european outlook states "their view of the world is not our view of the world, their laughter is not our laughter, their hurt is not our hurt." One of the best examples of this philosophy is the european "trade to Afrika", the slave trade. Most European writers on this period try to make the heinous traffic of human flesh appear as an almost harmless secondary factor which was essential to European colonial expansion. In other words what was good for them was very bad for us, which a careful study of history will show is usually the case. Even when the Europeans record Afrikan history, particularly in reference to Egypt, they have attempted to white wash us almost completely out of it. But thanks be to the Creator, we do not have to depend on them to find out who we really are and what our true place is in the history of the world. In these times we have been so abundantly blessed with a host of Black Scholars who have labored diligently to melt from the annuals of Earth the dross of white academia and bring forth the pure gold of an Afrikan World View.

An old Afrikan proverb tells the story of a little bird who used to fly everyday over a great expanse of jungle and upon attracting the attention of the inhabitants of a certain village relate the exploits of his victorious encounters with a strong and powerful male lion. One day a little boy inquired of his father saying, "Father, how can a little bird, such as this, overpower and defeat a great lion? This indeed is incredible. Could his story in fact be true?" The

5

father replied, "Son, we shall never know until one day the lion comes to our village and tells his story." Brothers and sisters let us go on to tell our-story.

Unfortunately there is the unpleasant reality that portions of our history are somewhat intertwined and connected with that of the European. This is a natural, or shall we say, unnatural occurance in the ease of the evolution of the whites, since the Black Man is the first and the originator of everything of true value on the planet Earth. Following is the story of how the barbaric inhabitants emerged from the caves of Europe, immigrated to England and eventually became the British Empire, as seen through the eyes of the Black Man.

Chapter Two

Ancient Afrikan Scientists Bring Civilization to the British Isles

CHAPTER TWO

ANCIENT AFRIKAN SCIENTISTS BRING CIVILIZATION TO THE BRITISH ISLES

BLACK DOMINATION IN THE ANCIENT WORLD

The European usually refers to things which happened before his time, that is before he began to develop the skills to record and tell "his-story", as being "prehistoric" and he interprets these events in terms of his mean cave dwelling existence at the dawn of his civilization. But what was the world really like in those remote times? In most ancient days the continent of Afrika and what was later to become known as Asia, America and Europe and all of the continents were joined together into one great land mass. One need but look at a map of the world to see how the pieces of the geographical puzzle were once joined together [1] At that time there was a wonderful Eden-like climate which pervailed all over the globe. These mild climatic conditions were essentially tropical. All over the world even as far as Greenland and the Arctic Circle fossils of elephants, hippopotami, rhinoceroses, camels, lions and other animals indigenous to a tropical latitute have been discovered. During that period the earth is described as having been a thriving luxuriant tropical paradise with palm trees, magnolias, sequoias and myriad other flourishing trees and plants. Where ever coal is found or mined from the earth even in the coldest regions is indicative of a once tropical climate. [2]

Who were the inhabitants who peopled the earth amid these paradisiacal conditions? How did they look in physical appearance? Well, it is a known fact that indigenous tropical man is never white, he is Black or dark brown with a flat nose, frizzly woolen hair, protruding jaw or some variation of a ebony hue. [3] Many modern day anthropologists like L.S.B. Leakey as well as the Bible agree that man originated in a tropical environment. [4] J.A. Rogers says "recent discovery seems to indicate that the negro element preceeded the white and yellow everywhere. . .the original color of primitive man was black. . .these earliest known human beings of whom we have fairly abundant evidence from their skeletons and their art on all the continents might have lived anywhere from 600,000 to 8,000 B.C." [5] As regards these Afrikans Rogers goes on to further state "what became of the negro inhabitants of Europe no one can say they were

7

there before the great ice age and they disappeared. . ."[6]

At the end of the last ice age in Europe around or before 11,000 B.C.E.* the great land mass including Atlantis was separated by what many scientist refer to as the "continental drift" this caused a detachment of the American, European and Asian continents and the islands of the sea from Afrika which was the heart and center of all the land mass. At this time there also occured the severing of the land bridge between the British Isles and the European mainland. As the effects of the last Ice Age in Northern Europe began to subside the climate in the southern and western parts of the continent gradually became warmer and warmer but in the north the coldness of the snow, ice and fog remained intense, that is why the early caucasian inhabitants of the region far north of Europe were so backwards for such a long period of time and ran millennia behind the rest of the world in the development of human civilization. This post-Ice Age period along with the general harsh condition of northern Europe in those remotest times is largely responsible for the formation of the caucasians' dog-eat-dog mentality and that zenophobic warlike characteristic which is so prevalent in his culture even unto this day.

While the nordics to the far north of the European continent were crippled by the cold and the scarceness of food and game, the Black Man in southern Afrika was flourishing in his tropical surroundings and making great advances in the art of toolmaking, agriculture, ironsmelting and other technical sciences while at the same time laying the basis for the collective benefits of a homogenous society. This Afrikan, from his centers of culture in the heartland of the Mother Continent, spread throughout Alkebulan up into Europe, Asia and all over the earth carrying with him the rejuvenating sciences of a neo-civilization. [7] The Black Man's history goes so far back in antiquity that dates become just a matter of reference for convenience. When rightly understood, for us there is no real beginning or ending "for there never was a time when the Black Man was not and there will never be a time when the Black Man will cease to be."

Sometime after the Ice Age in Europe a pale "weak savage race without laws or cultivation of any thought, destitute of memory and too devoid of understanding even to conceive hope began to evolve in the far north. At this time the Black Race which is far more ancient than the whites was dominant on the earth and held the sceptre of science and power. . . ." [8] All over the world there exists incalculable members of monuments, rock paintings and arts and crafts which bear the generous features of the Afrikan physiognomy.

8

They have existed from the most ancient of times even unto this day, bearing silent witness as sentinels of the grandeur and social state of the mighty Black Men and Women who once covered the face of the Earth Higgins says "Nearly all of the ancient gods of the old and new world were Black and had wooly hair. . .all the wood and stone deities were Black. They remain as they were first made in very remote times. . . ." [9] Even the Bible refers to the ancient image of the Creator as being "the color of amber" and "with haid like lamb's wool." [10]

THE MIGHTY BLACK MEN FROM ALKEBULAN

Around about 12,000 B.C.E. another wave of Black Men came up out of the southern portion of Africa and spread their culture to all corners of the world including Asia, southern and western Europe and is believed in some scientific circles to have spread across the Atlantic into the Americas. The giant Afrikanoid images carved into huge stone boulders that are so profusely disseminated over South America, the Easter Islands and other islands of the sea apparently bear witness of this and other similiar events. This "uninterrupted belt" of Afrikan high culture with southern Alkebulan at its axis stretched all the way from the America's through Central Europe, India, Central Asia and unto the foot of the Caucasus Mountains. [11] During this time of universal Afrikan sovereignty, the Black Man established his religious centers in cyclopean cities all over the world. The stately, brilliant and powerfully built Nubian type Ebony Man who had dominated the Earth with his wisdom and enlightenment for countless centuries eventually encountered the violent and contentious white Neanderthal and Cro-magnon cave men from the far north who were dense, stubborn and impervious to his high civilization and culture, as a result of incessant conflicts with these club bearing warlike creatures the Afrikan withdrew from Europe to the peaceful surroundings of the Mother Continent and other tropical areas in the world. This mighty Black Man described by Dr. Diop as "tall, with an extremely high skull (that is a large cranial capacity for an ample brain) is designated Grimaldi by European archaeologists and anthropologists, this being so because of the numerous remains and artifacts first found in modern times in a cave in Grimaldi, Italy. [12] Many relics of this Brother called Grimalde have been dug up in England where he lived from about 10,000 to 8,000 B.C.E.. When the Nubian-Grimaldi first invaded southern Europe bearing the emblem of the dragon on his standard and wielding the awesome spectacle of fiery torches, an element yet unknown to the ape-like white Neanderthal and Cro-magnon, the caucasian fled in abject terror before him and retreated back up into the far recesses of the inclimate north.[13]

The Nubian-Grimaldi was later succeeded in Europe by his shorter brother, in physical though not in mental statute, commonly referred to in scientific circles as the negrito.[14] These little Black Men who came to be dubbed by later Greek historians as Iberians, so named after the Ebro River in Spain the center of their cultural activities in Europe, were the first known inhabitants of Spain and Portugal after the evacuation of the Nubian-Grimaldi. These Iberians are described as being short, swarthy (the German word for Black) wooley haired, robust and "dolichocephalic" (long-headed) and their women of whom many statuette Venuses have been found all over Europe as "steotopygic" - that is to say one who bears a large, healthy posterior. Some of these physical characteristics were retained in the strong Afrikan strain of many of the later European people of the Andalusian Peninsula (Southern Spain) which was reinforced some twenty-two centuries later by the Blackamoors who conquered the region, occasioning some geographers to declare that "Afrika begins at the Pyrenees" (a group of mountains separating Spain from France).[16]

From their base of operations in Spain then called "Iberian Ethiopia"[16] this particular group of Afrikans sometimes called the Celti-Iberians or Black Celts[17] migrated east to the Caucasus Mountains in Russia and west to the British Isles around 3,000 B.C.E.. When they arrived in England they brought with them the hieralpha which was a plowshare used to till the earth. Apparently these agrarian people must have had a very sacred regard for the land for the designation "hieralpha" is from the Ethiopian words "heir" meaning "holy" and "alpha" meaning "one". Along with the agricultural sciences they also brought the art of tool and pottery making, the mining technologies of iron, tin, copper, silver and salt. They were deeply devoted to strong family structures and loved to pass their leisure in singing and dancing. The Iberians spoke a language closely related to the Egyptian and Cushite tongues which many Europeans scholars have often misnomered Hamitic or Semitic. These Afrikans also wrote a distinct alphabet of twenty-eight characters very similar to that of another Afrikan people known as Phoenicians.[18]

Between 2,000 and 1,500 B.C.E. wandering bands of Scythians from the Rhine and Danube River regions of mainland Europe began migrating to England, these pale faced intruders from

10

the north began making war with the Iberians and finally took control of the trade routes. Many of the swarthy Iberians migrated to Wales on the western shore of Britian, most of them returned to Spain, some remained in England and lived side by side with the white savages who commandeered unto themselves the name and culture of their Black predecessors. Those who chose to stay were eventually assimilated into the Celtic-Gallic ethnology. Thus began the slow decline of the Afrikan-Iberian culture in Britian.

BUILDERS OF THE FIRST

Once again around 2,800 B.C.E. a group of cyclopean builders, descendants of the original rulers of the planet Earth whom Rogers calls "Cushites" from which he says is derived the terminology "Celts" came to England and built the gargantuan structure of Stonehenge.[19] These wise Black Giants from Afrika built many similiar structures all over the world, 127 have been found in Europe thus far. On many of these buildings and even cities are inscribed the journey of the celestial spheres, the path of the constellations, the cycles of the seasons and many other scientific insignia. These giants among men sometimes represented in ancient art with three eyes, the third eye being symbolic of great spiritual wisdom and humane benevolence, possessed great mechanical skills and an in depth knowledge of astronomy as evidenced by the cyclical formations of the cities and the huge stones used in most of their buildings, such as those at Stonehenge in England.

These profound scholars and architects who were priests of the Ancient Afrikan Mystery System[20] are ignorantly portrayed as monsters with one eye in the center of their forehead in the European corruption of Afrikan theology and high science into Greco-Roman mythology. The Greeks, even after centuries of tutoring by the Afrikan, could not fully comprehend the true meaning and practical application of Mystery School symbolism. Yet as late as 16th Century Europe one elemental truth about the cyclops was retained by the Italian artist Ercole de Roberti.[21] He portrayed the cyclops as being Black with large heads.

According to the Encyclopedia Britannica an excess of some 600 structures of various materials and sizes yer similiar in formation and contemporary to Stonehenge have been discovered in England and western France.[22] Some European scholars claim that Stonehenge and other resembling structures were built by an unknown people. They do this to avoid admitting that these ancient monuments were built by Black Men rather than white men. One

English historian, Gerald Massey, says that Stonehenge was build by a Black architect named Morien from Egypt. In fact Massey has devoted many of his writings to "Egyptian origins in the British Isles." [23] Godfrey Higgins in *Anacalypsis*, Volume I states that Stonehenge was a temple of the Black curly head Buddha of India and Egypt. This is probably true because from remotest times the religion of the "One", the "Unmoved Mover", or as is sometimes referred to as the "Om" of which Buddha was one of the many incarnate representations, was universally practiced by Black People all over the face of the Earth.[24] Other findings seem to indicate that Stonehenge was also used as a university setting for the priest-teachers and their students as well as a place of ritual theatre which was a dramatic enactment of ancient religious themes and principles. This ancient monument was also used as an astronomical observatory.

Stonehenge is the most noted of the many structures built by cyclopean giants from Afrika during the so-called prehistoric times on the Salisbury Plains in Wilkshire located in the southern portion of England. Investigative studies have shown that the positions of the hugh stone slabs used in its construction are precisely connected by sockets and joints, indicating a very advanced technology. These slabs signify the places on the celestrial horizon where the sun and moon rise and set about the time of the summer solstice (June 21st) and winter solstice (December 21st). The summer solstice marks the place of the sun when the Northern Hemisphere of Planet Earth (North Pole) slants towards it. This is the longest day in the year. The winter solstice indicates the place of the sun when the Northern Hemisphere (North Pole) gradually slants away from it. This is the shortest day of the year. Some of the huge stones used in the construction of Stonehenge appear to have been brought to the building site from a quarry some 300 miles away in the western parts of Wales. Obviously these Afrikans were highly skilled technicians, mathematicians and engineers to move stones weighing 50 tons or more over that stretch of ground.

This marvelous feat calls our attention to similiar massive building projects which were taking place some 6,000 miles away in Ethiopia and Egypt during this same era. No doubt the builders of Stonehenge and the builders of the pyramids and temples in Afrika were once classmates at the University of Luxor and affiliates of the same scientific societies. While the pyramids were built in a triangular fashion, the Stonehenge was built in a circular formation, one of the symbols and insignias of the priestly builders was the 360 degree circle with a pyramid within its diameter and the all

12

seeing eye of Osiris in the midst of the pyramid. Thus we see the continuity of our Ancient High Culture as it spread from one end of the planet to the other.

The outer circle of Stonehenge consisted of thirty grey stone blocks weighing 50 tons each and standing 13½ feet above ground measuring a collective diameter of 97 feet. A continuous circle of smaller slabs were placed and perfectly jointed on top of them. The inner circles consisted of about 60 blue stones and within this diameter were 2 horseshoe shaped sets of stones, one inside the other, opening towards the northeast. In the middle of the inner horseshoe was a flat 16 foot sandstone altar. A huge marker stood 80 yards east of the altar set in such a way as to cast a shadow on the altar at dawn on the day of the summer solstice. Stonehenge with its ancient Egyptian markings also served as an excellent astronomical calendar of which the seasons of the year and the eclipses of the sun and the moon could be accurately predicted by the brilliant Black scientists who built it. Also in that same area in England is a wooden monument very similiar in structure to Stonehenge built around 3,000 years ago.

In North and South America there have been found similiar structures built by its indigenous inhabitants such as the Bighorn Medicine Wheel discovered in Wyoming. This wheel was used by the aborigine for astronomical cipherings. In fact wherever people of color have dwelt in the world, which is just about everywhere, evidences of these type structures have been found. [25] Surely the Black Man, in his original spiritual and mental state, is the beginning and the end, the end and the beginning, the Alpha and the Omega, the first and the last and the first again, 360 degrees of eternity, the manifestation and revelation of the power and the glory of the Creator on Earth. When we come to the light of the understanding of this glorious truth, there will be no power on earth that will be able to stop or contain us. The Black Race is being summoned by the Divine Forces of Life unto the mark of a higher calling which is hidden in the depths of the very universe itself. As we become One with ourselves and each other then we will become one with the One. Therein is the true meaning of our existence as a People.

MINI-CHRONOLOGY

Now let us piece together the motley of anthropological and archeological facts we have just garnered and digested from the foregoing information. In light of the present data this is the picture which comes to mind. In the beginning all of the continents were joined together in one great land mass. The Earth was tropical, with an even temperature averaging between 75 and 78 degrees producing an abundance of food, luxurious plant life, gold, silver, and precious stones with the sweet fragrance of inumerable flowers which covered the great land mass in opulent abundance. [26] Amid this paradise the original man, the Black Man, dominated the Earth in all his glory and magnificence. From his cultural center in the southern portion of Afrika [27] he fanned out in all directions establishing the Eden High Culture, of which Atlantis was a part, over the face of the whole Earth. [28]

In the course of time according to the many traditions, folklore, scriptures and sacred books scattered throughout the world, the original man somehow came to a parting of the way with the laws of nature and its Creator thus he began to lose his power on the Earth, hence the story of the fall of man as related in the book of Genesis in the Bible. [29] The Genesis Scroll which is so profusely permeated with the symbolism of Mesopatamian and Egyptian Mythology and legend is more a colorful story to illustrate a principle than a detailed record of all the facts. [30] Sometime after this epic event, which is the subject of numerous traditions in the world of color reported to have taken place at various geographical locations around the globe, there occurred the continental drift, followed by the Ice Age and its attendant inter-galacial epochs which came to pass in Europe and the northern hemispheres of Asia and the American continent. [31]

Around 30,000 B.C.E. the ice from the last glacial assault on Europe was in the last stages of its recess. It was about this time that Blacks again migrated from the southern portion of Alkebulan and began the long evolutionary process of reestablishing civilization there. [32] The bitter cold and fogginess of Central Europe and the British Isles retarded the normal rate of cultural acceleration in that area, nevertheless the Afrikans who settled in Europe during this period, as if being obsessed with the idea of reclaiming their former universal glory power, tenaciously continued through their intermittent migrations the quest to upgrade that portion of the world. Eventually they realized a degree of success during the Bronze Age (circa 15,000 B.C.E.).

Meanwhile far off up in the ice and snow covered regions of northern Europe there evolved and emerged a strange albino mutant-type which came to be manifested in the raw meat eating and violent club wielding pale Neanderthal and Cro-magnon cave dwellers so often referred to in the white man's record of his "prehistoric times." As these wild untamed creatures poured down like roving

14

beasts, shouting inarticulate guttural sounds such as "ugh" and "umph" they spread their savagery and canine contentious way of life like a herpetic infection through central, eastern and western Europe, robbing, stealing, diffusing disease and murdering everything in their path. These are the forebearers of the modern day Caucasian race. Once again the Afrikan embarked on a campaign of neo-civilization, invaded Europe in the person of the fire bearing Nubian-Grimaldi and conquered the undeveloped and retarded apeman, driving them back up into the far recesses of the north across the Baltic Sea and the Caucasus Mountains. Several thousand years later the Grimaldi are followed by a wave of little Black Men known as Iberians who come from their High Culture centers in southeast Alkebulan and settle in the southernly portions of eastern and western Europe. From their base of operations in Spain and France they emigrate across the English Channel to the British Isles. There the Iberians established a long (over 6,000 years) and generally peaceful agragrian society based on the principles and values of their Afrikan Ancestors, while keeping constant communications with their learned brothers and sisters in Alkebulan (the oldest known designation of the Mother continent).

This mini-chronology is not intended on our part to be an invasion of the field of anthropology (the study of the origins of man) and its attendant disciplines but rather an attempt to simplify and make digestible to the layman the confused hodge-podge of dates, charts and chronologies so often concocted by some of the devotees to this field of study. One thing is for certain - as is clearly stated in Dr. Chancellor Williams' monumental work *The Destruction of Black Civilization* - there is a great need for more and more Afrikans to embark upon the disciplines of anthropology, archeology, languistics and other social science fields which are so totally dominated by Europeans today. Blacks are sorely needed in these specialized areas of study and research to set the record straight and to present their findings to the Black Masses from an Afrikan World View. Fortunately in relationship to this most important factor many trails have already been blazed by such brilliant scholars as Dr. Cheikh Anta Diop, Yusef ben Jochannon (affectionately known to his students as Dr. Ben), John G. Jackson, Ivan Van Sertima and a host of other Black sages opening before us a whole new world of exciting and fascinating study. Afrikans of this caliber have made the times in which we are now living one of the most glorious ages of scholarship and academia since the days of Afrika's golden age in ancient Ethiopia and Egypt. You would be wise, my beloved Black brothers and sisters, to take full advantage of this great body of knowledge and avail yourself of its life giving benefits by attending every lecture and purchasing all the books and documents that your time and resources will allow.

Now let us sum up this presentation of the life and times of the "builders of the first" by way of a diagrammed profile of epochs and dates being ever careful to keep in mind that whenever you reach this far back in history, dates and chronology are merely convenient guidelines to aid one in his frame of reference. Therefore the following dates are approximates and not definites.

1,800,000 B.C.E.*	Zenjanthropus-Boysie (Man of the black coast) found in the Olduvai Gorge, Kenya, East Afrika, believed by many anthropologists to be the oldest remains of early man. [33]
600,000 - 8,000 B.C.E.	Total Black domination of the world.
100,000 - 70,000 B.C.E.	Homo hablis (handy man) discovered in East Afrika by one of the Black members of L.S.B. Leakey's anthropological staff. The environment of the homo hablis is reputed to have been more physically and technologically advanced than anywhere else in the world at that time.
30,000 B.C.E.	Iron smelting in southern Afrika - new wave of Black migrations to Europe from Alkebulan.
20,000 B.C.E.	Violent encounters with the pale Neanderthal and Cro-magnons.
12,000 B.C.E.	The arrival of the Nubian-Grimaldi in Europe.
8,000 B.C.E.	End of the Old Stone Age - arrival of the Iberians in the British Isles.
2,848 B.C.E.	Revitalization of the Stonehenge building project.
2,000 B.C.E.	The warlike Scythians emerge from the caves

16

of the Caucasus Mountains and begin to stir up trouble in middle Europe.

1,500 B.C.E.   The barbaric Nordics from the north driven by the pressure of the Scythians hordes from the northeast invade the Iberian civilizations in eastern and central Europe. The encroaching whites conquer the peaceful, domestic Iberians and co-opt their name and as much of their culture as the dullness of the Caucasians mind of that day would permit. Most of the Celti-Iberians repatriate back to their homeland in Afrika. Many of them immigrated westward joining their brothers in the British Isles. Some few others remained in Spain, Portugal, France and central Europe carrying on a valiant struggle to maintain the quality of life that was created by their high civilization.

This in brief is our chronological review of the acts and deeds of "the builders of the first" as set forth in this chapter.

* Instead of the usual B.C. (before Christ), A.D. (Anno Domini - in the year of our Lord) method of dating applied by European chroniclers we prefer the more accurate system developed by our own Dr. Yosef ben Jochannon, B.C.E. - before the Christian Era, C.E. - Christian Era. The idea of applying the approximate birth of Jesus ben Joseph commonly known as Jesus Christ as a point of reference for the recording of historical events was first introduced in the year 532 C.E. by Dionysius Exiguus, a Roman Catholic priest who lived during the reign of Justinian I. Unfortunately Dionysius was at least three to six years short on accuracy in his calculations. That is why it is more precise to refer to this pivotal device as before and during the Christian Era.

Chapter Three

They Came and Things Have Never Been the Same

THEY CAME AND THINGS HAVE NEVER BEEN THE SAME

WHERE DID THEY COME FROM?

According to Dr. Diop Blacks were the only humans on the planet Earth until the 4th galacial epoch (Ice Age). [34] This proves a real embarrassment for most European scholars for it brings to the fore questions of their origins as a race and the fact of their elongated barbaric state as a people since that origin. The most obvious questions are where did white folks come from? And what are the causes which brought them about?

As regards these questions on the origin of the white race many theories have been advanced of which limited space will not permit us to examine here in this particular work. However we will consider three of the most commonly known explanations. Firstly, dark skinned men who migrated to the far north of the European continent immediately after the 3rd Ice Age about 100,000 years ago eventually experienced an alteration of the pineal gland which caused them to lose their original pigmentation. Through the millenia of recessive genetic evolution the early traces of their Afrikan humanity diminished and these bleached out mutant creatures became the immediate ancestors of the Caucasian race. [35]

After living for tens of thousands of years in this icy, sunless, and foggy environment the new species was cast in a dull almost catatonic state, devoid of understanding and prone to incessant violence. Secondly, some say the pale ones were cast aways from another planet and being confined here by extra-terrestrial powers proceeded by force of violence and trickery to gradually take control of the Earth from the original Black Man. Thirdly, there is the story of Yakub (Jacob) as set forth by the Nation of Islam, under the guidance of the Messenger which states in essence that the white race is the demonic creation of Dr. Yakub, a renegade scientist from the High Culture Civilization of the original Black Man. For a clearer view of this doctrine read *Message To The Black Man* by Elijah Muhammad. Notwithstanding any of the concepts of how or why they arrived here. The irrefutable fact of the matter is whites have always been alien and destructive to the spiritual, mental and physical well being of the original Black Man every since they first appeared on the planet.

18

In light of the foregoing some Black Folks who are dead set on trying to save the white race may be prompted to pose the question? Does this not prove that the white man is our brother? The answer is most emphatically no. In *The Cultural Unity of Black Africa,* Dr. Cheikh Anta Diop states, "the peoples who lived for a lengthy period of time in their place of origin were molded by their surroundings in a durable fashion." [36] Note Diop's use of the word "durable" which comes from the Latin "durus" meaning "hard and set in its way". In other words you cannot change a thing that is not real. The Caucasian race even if they were distantly descendant from the progeny of the original Black Man is, by virtue of the harsh, barren and cold regions in which they evolved, a new and distinct species "hard set" in their "unchangable" nature and as such cannot scientifically be considered the genetic brothers of the Afrikan Race. Some may hysterically declare this a terrible thing to say about the white man and that it smacks of bigotry and hatred but is the Black Man's recognition of this inescapable fact a pronouncement of "racism in reverse"? Of course not. This conclusion is arrived at through painstaking research and analysis and should be subjected to deducible reasoning rather than sentimental emotionalism.

In this same treatise Diop further implies that the brotherhood of man theory is at best an idealized fantasy of the triumph of universal humanism. Throughout this same work, he clearly delineates the xenophobic mania of the Caucasian which engenders in him a fear and hatred of all strangers in contrast to the xenophilous nature of the Afrikan which motivates him towards the love and trust of strangers. This characteristic love of mankind trait on the part of Blacks has during the panoramic course of history, since our first encounter with the pale creatures from the north, often been used against us. [37] In spite of the fact that from time to time throughout the recorded annals of ancient history whites are reported to have worshipped Black People as gods. [38,] The innate schizoid, paranoid and envious disposition of the Caucasian was variously ignited by their basic fear and hatred of other humans especially peoples of color. This xenophobia is very deeply embedded in the psyche of the European and is the main cause of his violent, aggressive and warlike nature. [39] On the other hand the reason why the love and respect xenophilia of the Afrikan has tended to work against him whenever he dwelt in societies controlled by Europeans, is that the Caucasians greatest desire is to eternally dominate the Black Man. In ancient days as well as in so called modern times whenever Black and whites came into contact with each other generally there was the catalytic reaction of chaos and conflict. That is why the two races will forever be irreconcilable. In harmony with this fact Lou Palmer in *Black Books Bulletin* quotes Dr. Chancellor Williams' profound declaration thusly,

> "The necessary reeducation of Blacks and a possible solution of racial crisis can begin, strangely enough, only when Blacks fully realize this central fact in their lives: the white man is their bitter enemy. This is not the ranting of wild-eyed militancy, but the calm and unmistakeable verdict of several thousand years of documented history." [40]

Even from the remotest times in Caucasian Europe where the populace primarily lived on flesh, milk and cheese, each man's neighbor was considered to be his enemy - robbery, theft and vandalism outside the boundary of one's immediate habitat was approvingly looked upon as a normal way of life. [41] Affirming this fact the *Encyclopedia Britannica* states, "Each man saw an enemy in his nearest neighbor; war was a normal condition, not only between groups that differed one from another in custom and language. . . but also and even more frequently, between little neighboring tribes who were conscious of a common origin. . ." [42]

THE IRRECONCILABLE OPPOSITES

Perhaps ideally it really would be nice if the two races could live side by side in harmony and peace but time and history has proven that the diverse natures of Blacks and whites are just not compatible. The Afrikan and Caucasian travel on insulated wave lengths on two distinct and separate paths that can never be joined together. Whenever the chemistry of the two are forced into proximity the results are always volatile. This is best exemplified by the Afrikan and European diametrical approach to life, death and sexuality, for instance the cross which was originally a symbol of life to the Blacks became a symbol of death to the whites and is now a graveyard ornament in western society. The epitome of European art is the crucifixion, a bleeding emaciated dead man hanging on a cross, a signification of the intense, guilt-ridden suicidal syndrome so prevalent in the Caucasians initial tragic outlook on life. The Europeans glorious acclaim of Shakespeare's tragedies and the present nuclear threat of the atom, hydrogen and neutron bombs is also indicative of the white man's true nature. [43] As concerning human sexuality the original Black Man and Woman conceived of

20

this as a revelation of the Divine Energy Force, a holy experience, a thing of insurpassable beauty, the Eternal Fire which when related to in its proper context would inspire them to enhance the quality of life, To the white man it was a lewd, nasty and sinful, bestial passion as was later demonstrated in the European religious ideologies of Roman Catholicism and Puritanism, the confused, warped, imbalanced and pathological attitude toward sexuality on the part of whites is further demonstrated in the almost social acceptance of rape today in modern European society. [44'] In essence what is manifestly exhibited here by these few brief examples above is; what means good to us means evil to them and what is good for them is usually bad for us. As Minister Louis Farrakhan so beautifully put it "the white man's heaven is the Black Man's hell". [45]

To the Original Man and most other people of color a solid family structure was the most sacred entity in the world. The Afrikan male had a strong affection for women and children and his exalted view of the Black Woman was based on her particular place in the development of civilization. Therefore the Black Man reputed it his primary duty to protect her, the children she bore and the society she nourished. When we speak of the exalted accord of the Ancient Black Man toward his woman this does not mean that sisters of today should spiritually, physically or mentally put a price tag on themselves as if they were some kind of commodity, but rather carry themselves in the respectful manner and modest deportment worthy of their original and rightful station in life. Unfortunately some brothers hearing me speak on this subject of the divine sanctity of the Mother of civilization have expressed some degree of anxiety in this matter with marked concern for the looseness, masochism and present state of mind exhibited by many sisters today and how it becomes very difficult to comprehend the Black Woman in her proper light. But I say unto you my brothers that it is the responsibility of the Black Man to lead those sisters who are caught up into this negativity out of that state of being and to set a good example by the way he personally treats Black Women, for as long as the world can disrespect your woman it will never have any respect for you as a man. If perchance you find some sisters unresponsive to your positive attitude towards them then you must be strong and conduct yourself the way you know the Original Man should. Above all do not allow yourself to react to the infantile insecurities that to a greater or lesser degree victimizes most Black People - male and female. A steadfast determination on the part of brothers and sisters to carry themselves as adult men and women, who instead of

21

villifying each other about their short comings will preferably and intelligently work to solve their problems together is the only way that we will emerge victorious. Remember the disparaging feelings that many Black People have towards each other is the result of a long conditioning process. As Jesus said, "an enemy has done this." Nevertheless it is up to us to break the bonds and create a new and positive life style. This is not the sentimentality of starry eyed idealism but rather the stating of a most important contributing factor to our survival and advancement as a people.

Even though the roles of the male and female throughout the history of the Black experience were often criss-crossed especially since the Euro-Asian invasion of Afrika, the slave trade and the madness of today's world. The basic original attitude of the Afrikan man and Women, who were the builders of the best and highest civilizations ever known to man must be reawakened within us and demonstrated in the way we do things within the fabric of our daily lives. Anything short of this will continue to perpetrate the confusion and degeneracy so prevelant in our midst today particularly in the areas of perverted sexual orientation such as homosexuality, freakism, etc. which further endanger the Black Family structure. Above all while collectively seeking to find solutions to our problems the Black Man and Woman must not see each other as the enemy. But more correctly we must out of necessity band together to win victory over our natural enemy, the one who views every good thing we do as a threat to his existance as evidenced by his mad compulsion to control, define, and co-opt every aspect of our lives and in particular the Black Male-Female relationship.

From earliest times in Afrikan society there has always been a strong bond between mother and child. In our High Culture Societies to show disrespect to one's mother is tantamount to sacrilege. To the Afrikan the maternal instinct is the primary basis for a civilized society and provides the impetus to the paternal instinct which enables a man to see himself as more than just an axe swinger and a spear thrower. This attitude on the part of Blacks in the ancient world generated their very high regard for the Black Woman as the Queen of the Universe. [46] In stark contrast to this was the Europeans general lack of esteem for family and the feminine gender. To the nomadic Caucasian, family was a burden, he only loosely maintained out of the necessity to ensure the progeny of his race. [47] Infanticide was a common practice among the whites from remotest times even down to the Greco-Roman period. Diop reports "The abandonment of children and the burial of infant girls, considered as useless mouths to feed, were common practices throughout the whole patriarchal Eurasian world. . ." When Europeans first encountered the Afrikan they were astoinished at his loving affection for all of his children male and female alike. [48]

The existence of females in European society was further jeopardized by virtue of the fact that the Caucasian man held the power of life and death over his woman and children whom he could buy and sell at will. This misogynistic attitude on the part of the white man toward the white woman was carried forth into later European life when the so-called Christian holy men considered woman to be "an evil enemy of the faith and the gateway to hell." [49] The already perilous position of the woman in the ancient European societal structure was further burdened by the practice of polyandry which amounted to little more than gang rape of the woman by the men in her family and community. [50]

THE AFRIKAN FAMILY STRUCTURE

It would be a negligent oversight to examine the Afrikan family structure without making reference to polygyny (the practice of several women joining unto one man), which incidently was first introduced into ancient societies by the Afrikan Woman. In the old days of Afrika's glory the woman considered herself nothing without a man to defend her and a man was nothing without a woman and a family to defend. At this time polygyny was generally practiced throughout most of the world, a result of the Black Man's cultural influence all around the globe. Polygyny or polygamy, as some call it, was adopted by Black Women to ensure every woman in the society having access to a man, whose primary role was protector, guide, provider and keeper of the realm. [51]

As already stated, in these ancient Afrikan societies women were held in the highest honor and respect, the female entity was revered and oft-times worshipped as the Great Mother, Nourisher and Sustainer of life, the source of all terrestrial inspiration and the maintainer of revitalized life. This was the usual way of life in those wonderful days when the Black Man dominated the earth, widespread love, respect and affection was consistently demonstrated by the Black Man to the Black Woman. He delighted in adorning her with gold and silver often rhapsodizing to her in the most beautiful language (perhaps this is why sisters still love to hear a Black Man lay down some good "rap" even unto this day), the norm in ancient Black Society, where each gender clearly accepted and dignified their distinguished roles in the community was a mutual affection and

23

respect for one another.[52] In those days of amorous joy Black Women delighted in dancing and singing praises to their men especially after they had returned from the battle (usually in defense of the homeland) or the hunt.

The family practices of the Black Man's High Culture System began to deteriorate in certain parts of the world namely Europe and northern Asia when the Caucasian appeared on the scene. At first white Europeans with no real culture of their own, other than the insatiable love of warfare, tried to emulate the Afrikan in the practice of polygyny although there was no general change in his attitude regarding the treatment of the Caucasian woman. With the coming of syphilis and its wide-spread infections among the women of his race, which caused the largest percentage of the female population to die out like flies, the nomadic Caucasians leaving their bodies where they fell, the shortage in the already limited female population was intensified so the European shortly returned to monogamy, homosexuality and the wide-spread practice of polyandry - one woman, many men.[53] In the European custom of polyandry one woman, be she mother, daughter, sister and in some cases a queen, became the wife of as many as ten or more men, included in this group might be her father, her son, her brother, her cousin, her uncle as well as her husband and on certain occasions, at the whim of the family head man she was made available for the pleasure of all the men in the community. The ancient Europeans said their rationale for doing this was an attempt to minimize the constant fighting and bloodletting of rivals over the limited amount of women available.[54] It was out of this confusion that the patriarchal line of descent and the modern European system of monogamy was born. As a result of eventual European world domination many Black People and other peoples of color have been forced to adopt monogamy and in same cases rape and homosexuality as a cultural frame of reference. Subliminally this is one of the manifold reasons for the many traumatic Black Male-Female relationships in the United States and other parts of the world today. But in spite of this mental conditioning we as a people must join unto our own and through the proper light of understanding correctly put into practice those systems that will prosper and sustain us, insuring Our survival and longevity on the earth.

At this point a word of caution is in order. The above statements of historical fact - and it is an irrefutable fact that the practice of polygyny was the norm for Afrikans before the coming of the European - were not intended to denegrate or condemn those

24

families where the Black Man and Woman mutually prefer a monogamous relationship, rather they have been cited to present the cultural roots, validity and obvious advantages of polygyny for Black families who wish to practice it today. Of course it must be clearly understood, especially by the brothers that this is not something you just up and jump into without careful thought and preparation, for there are great responsibilities involved. But those Black Men and Women who are serious and adequately prepare themselves through consultation, study and self discipline applying the practice of polygyny on the high spiritual plane of which it was originally developed will eventually become some of the most respected and powerful men and women in the world. It is believed by some Black Scholars who have carefully and painstakingly studied the societal structures of Afrikan People that the correct application of this system could be a mighty key factor in the economic, spiritual, mental and physical survival of Blacks wherever we are in the world today.

One of the main reasons why polygyny was developed and practiced by the ancients was to enhance the economic power of the family, community and nation. Wherein a brother might achieve moderately well in a basic monoganous structure, he could maximize his efforts a hundred fold with the right combination of sister-wives. Bear in mind this idea was first introduced into the community by the women of the society. The biblical story of Jacob, the reputed father of the Israelite nation, mentions his four wives and how the first two brought the latter two into the family.[55] In this present Euro-centric dominated society which is adverse to our very nature, it is somewhat difficult for us to practice those traditions which are more in tuned with our cosmic vibrations. Therefore we must adopt the wisdom of the Kawaida doctrine which advises us to practice "tradition and reason" as we strive to create a new society, a better condition and a better world. There is much truth in the old adage "Where there is a will, there is a way."

As always it is imperative for us as a people to be constantly advancing in knowledge and understanding ever cultivating the habit of doing those things which contribute to our growth. Above all we must not allow ourselves to become stagnant or we will be like the sitting waters that provide a habitation and breeding ground for blood sucking mosquitoes which can be likened unto our natural enemy hovering overhead, ever ready to feed upon our spiritual being and suck out the life blood of our mind, buzzing about and laying the eggs of his degenerate society. Those brothers and sisters who may react to the above statements out of wild undiciplined emotion

25

instead of the logic and scientific analysis of a sound mind which was originally created and given to you for the purpose of deductive reasoning, we advise; investigate and examine before you rush forward to condemn. Black People must be very certain that the concepts and decisions on the part of both male and female regarding the practice of polygyny are based on knowledge, wisdom, logic and understanding rather than negative emotional reaction. In light of this let not the white-mindedness that to some degree has infected all of us be a stumbling block to our progress as a race.

In raising this issue we are fully aware that humans tend to see into a concept that which appeals to their own personal desires, therefore we do strongly urge this subject be approached with the right mental and spiritual attitude. For it is our fervent prayer that we as a people may soon move from a position of weak powerlessness to our own proper position of power and strength on the Earth. Again we admonish those brothers and sisters who are desirous of practicing polygyny to study and investigate it well, being certain to properly prepare themselves mentally, physically and spiritually so as to avoid the emotional pain and suffering which is repercussive of incorrect and clandestine dealings. At all times the brother must be honest, fair, wise and strong in order for the sisters to feel confident and secure in the relationship. In light of the wide percentage gap between the Black Female and Black Male population, particularly in America, sisters should adopt a cooperative spirit, while seeking ways to remedy this situation. Every Black Woman who needs and wants one should have a Black man. Remember the survival of the race is at stake here, not our uncontrolled emotions. As I review the great benefits of polygyny to our ancient societies I'm inclined, while at the same time considering our present position here in the western hemisphere, to propose that this way of life must be revived and redeveloped in this day but it must be done correctly and in harmony with good principles. There is much information and many living examples of this practice available to those who diligently seek it out.[56]

Again let us reaffirm that this subject was not presented to foment consternation or to cause brothers and sisters to throw up their defenses, "jump salty with each other" and become polarized into forming opposing camps but rather as a review and examination of a historical reality which has been a component of the Afrikan way of life from earliest times unto the present. We trust those few who may not be in agreement with us in this matter will not assume a hostile posture and discount all the other points of vital information in this book. And so with undying Black Love for all, we take leave of this discussion confident that all our readers who ponder it will understand the true spirit in which it was set forth. Surely the Creator who revealed the divine light of understanding to our Ancestors in the past is the best knower and the best doer. Now let us consider some of the other sharply contrasting, irreconcilable distinctions which eternally exist between the Afrikan and the Caucasian.

THE EUROPEAN'S LOVE OF WAR

As we have previously observed most things which took place during so called prehistoric times are still a mystery to the European because those events happened long before his recessive evolutionary process was complete and before he was eventually taught the skills that would enable him to record his world view that is "his-story". Now today having been touched by the civilizing hand of the Afrikan he seeks to explain away that which he does not understand by portraying the events of the ancient world in terms of his limited cultural concepts, such as the theory of evolution. The theory of the original man being descendant from the ape which is propounded with such great authority by white dominated anthropological and archeological societies is just that, a "theory", not an unchallengeable scientific fact. Within the confines of this theory the Black Man is usually placed at the bottom of the evolutionary ladder. Even the renown L.S.B. Leakey of the prestigious National Geographic Society was initially ostracized for daring to suggest that man's earliest beginnings were in East Afrika. This arrogant and beligerent attitude on the part of most white scholars is indicative of the lengths to which they are willing to go in their frenzied attempts to avoid recognizing the obvious - the Black Man is the Original Man who created the High Culture Systems of the ancient world.

The Europeans negative response to unequivocal scientific data is a subliminal throwback to the days of his early existence when he roamed the Earth as a warmongering nomad wreaking havoc and devastation in his wake, in those remote days as is even true today the Caucasian's supreme way of life was war.[57] According to the Greek historian Herodotus (circa 484 B.C.E.) this basic outlook on life was still prevelant among Europeans in his day. He says the Thracians, Scythians, Persians, Lydians and almost all barbrous nations, hold in less honor than their other citizens those who learn any art and their descendants were deemed such to be noble as abstained from handicrafts and particularly those who devote themselves to war. All the Greeks moreover have adopted

27

this notion.[58] Though the pursuit of warfare was true of many other primitive peoples in their baser state, to the early Europeans it was the sweet essence of life itself, hence the white man's life-death suicidal syndrome. In contrast to this savagery, Blacks were generally sophisticates more attuned to brotherhood than battle.[59']

Although from time to time Blacks did fight among themselves, war was not the most desirable way of life, even today's Black on Black crime, for which there is absolutely no justification, is usually motivated by economic circumstances or a passionate emotional response to a given situation rather than a permanent state of mind. In today's world the tide has been turned, many of Our People who dwell in the inner city slums of white controlled metropolises and are subjected to the violent images of the mass media have now become the desperate ones; clawing at each other like "crabs in a barrel" and almost throughly inculcated with the dog eat dog mentality of their former slave masters. But in the days gone by this was not so, in fact had it not been for the presence of the Original Black Man there would probably not have been anything worthy of ever being called a civilization to exist on the European continent. In all likelihood due to their violent warlike culture the Europeans with their suicidal and guilt ridden syndrome without the civilizing hand of Afrika would have killed each other off - in mass extermination, which as harsh as it may seem may have been just as well since the Caucasian has been little more than a nuisance and source of conflict since his first appearance in the far north of Europe so many ages ago.

THE SCYTHIAN DISEASE

In this capsulized sketch of the Scythians, who were the progeny of the white Cro-magnon and the ancestors of Hitler's Aryan race, we are presenting a case study of the manifest abysmal gap between the Afrikan and the Caucasian who later invaded and inhabited east, west, central and southern Europe. With the hope that you will not accuse us of being "racial bigots teaching hatred" we are basing the following remarks on one white man's view of his own ancestry, a Greek geographer and historian of the 5th Century B.C.E. named Herodotus.

The Scythians were a branch of the Caucasian race from the far northeast of the Asian continent and parts of northern Europe. They referred to themselves as being the youngest of all the nations in the ancient world, having emerged on the scene somewhere between 2,000-1,500 B.C.E.[60'] According to one Scythian tradition they descended from a cave-dwelling "viper woman" a horrid creature with the head and torso of a woman from the waist up and the venom laden body of a shake from the buttocks down.[61] The story goes on to tell how she once tricked an Egyptian named Heracles into cohabiting with her and from this nefarious union was born three male freaks one of which became, so the story goes, the founder of the Scythian nation.[62'] In ancient times such colorful tales as this were employed as a method to illustrate a principle or the occurance of an actual event, although some of the details such as names, places, and physical descriptions used in the spinning of the yarn might be fantastic, nevertheless it was a very effective way of retelling an event or experience which held some importance to a people. A model example of this can be found in today's modern audio-visual media systems of movies and television where sometimes a presentation is preceeded by the statement "the story you are about to hear is true but the names have been changed to protect the innocent." In this instance the storytelling technique was applied to describe the origin of the widespread epidemic of syphilis among the Scythians.[63]

According to Rogers " The white plague, like syphilis, is a white man's disease. . .So far as in known, it originated in Europe.".[64] He further states that "ancient Egyptian civilization lasted for at least 5,000 years but no evidences of syphilis have been discovered there. . .the same was (and is) generally true of that part of Negro Afrika little touched by Arab or white civilization."[65] [Parentheses ours]

Homer, a Greek writer of about the 800's B.C.E. described the Scythians as dwelling in a remote place of mist and gloom, tremendously lacking in intelligence and civilization.[66] Herodotus says they were the most uncivilized nation in the world and sustained themselves by eating the raw flesh of their cattle.[67] In fact the eating of "rare" beef is still a big thing with their descendants here in America today, the rarer and bloodier it is, the better they like it. The Scythians also abhored the use of water for bathing instead they basked themselves in the vapors of burning hemp from which they would derive a narcotic high.[68] Herodotus further despicts them as violent, warlike nomads devoid in the science of agriculture who travelled and lived in wagons.[69]

These early predecessors of today's arrogant Euro-Americans rode into combat wearing black capes and fell upon their victims with vampire-like fury sucking the blood from the body of the first person they killed in battle.[70] It was also customary to scalp their fallen enemy and drink blood from his skull then adorning their

29

horses with the blood dripping scalps, they pranced about the camps howling victoriously, a custom later taught to the indigenous inhabitants of the American continent by pale-faced Europeans who talked with the forked tongue. [71] Whenever Scythians took prisoners of war they were relieved of their sight by a sizzling hot brand to the eyes.[72] The worst disgrace that a Scythian male could suffer was not to have had any dead enemies to his credit.[73] To these people war and violence were the paramount virtues and their highest act of worship was to sacrifice horses, cattle and humans to an iron sword, the symbol of their war god, over which the blood of the victims was poured.[74] This starving, desperate, syphilitic and destructive race of Scythians along with the Cimmerians and other roving bands of Indo-European nations were the ancestors of the Briton-Celts, Saxons, Jutes, Angles and other Germanic tribes who invaded and later settled in the British Isles.

THE INVASION OF THE BRITON-CELTS

We have already discussed the barbaric depraved mannerisms and attitudes of the early Caucasians and their descendants the Scythians. Now let us examine a more immediate ancestor of today's ultra-sophisticated Britisher, the white-Celt. Around 700 B.C.E. two great waves of tall blond headed Briton-Celts crossed from continental Europe into England. Their warriors who painted their bodies with a blue dye pushed the Iberians-Celts into the wild northern and western parts of the island. The Britons then occupied most of the area that is now England and Wales commandeering unto themselves the flourishing industry of the iron and tin mines formerly created by the Iberians. These Britons brought with them no culture of their own, they had no system of writing as did the Iberian-Celts who proceeded them nor did they strike coins, practice sculpture, painting or any other art form, in fact their culture never reached the level of the Iberians.

Many white historians confuse the Briton-Celts with the Iberians, referring to the whites as Celti-Iberians or Celto-Iberians and often misappropriating the culture and achievements of the Iberians who in fact were an Afrikan People to the Caucasian people whom they misnomer as Celts. Rogers suggests that the designations "Celts" is a European bastardization of the word "Cush" which Afrikans spell "Kush" the name of a High Culture center in the heart of Alkebulan, the land of the Blacks.[75] In the study of European history one must ever bear in mind that early whites having no culture of their own adopted the habit of assuming the names, languages, traditions and accomplishments of the indigeni which preceeded them in the lands they invaded and conquered. The origin of the Indo-European Briton-Celt can only be traced back to the late Iron Age period in Europe between 700 and 500 B.C.E.. They migrated from a center in ancient Gaul (France) and Germany over the English Channel into Britian.

To the civilized people of the Mediterrean world the Britons were barbarians well known for their ardent love of warfare and the effective use of iron weapons. By 85 C.E. the Romans had conquered all the Celtic lands except Ireland and northern Scotland. Most of the folklore of northern Europe such as Santa Claus, mistletoe, etc. is derived from the legends of the early Briton-Celts. See *Afrikan People and European Holidays: A Mental Genocide*, Book I, Chapter Six.

Chapter Four

Roman Legions Carry Afrikan Culture To Britain

ROMAN LEGIONS CARRY
AFRIKAN CULTURE TO BRITIAN

PRELUDE

While the remnants of the Black Iberians culture was being slowly destroyed in northwestern Europe it continued to flourish in the south, commonly referred to as the Mediterranean area. The Europeans who benefitted most from the civilizing hand of the Afrikan in this region were the Greeks and the Romans. That is why the Romans were so far ahead of other Europeans in culture and learning at the time of their arrival in Britian, for they had drank freely of the cup of knowledge passed down by the Blacks who preceeded them in the Mediterranean world. These were successively the Ethiopians, the Egyptians, the Cretans, the Phoenicians and the Egyptian colony of Ionia in Asia Minor. [76]

In this short elucidation on the Roman conquest of Britian we will reveal how all the information being set forth in this section ties into the history of the Fourth of You-Lie. For instance when the Americans seceded from Britian they adopted the Roman Senate as a model for their governing legislative body hence the United States Senate. In 1782 Congress adopted the eagle as the symbol of their new nation just as the Romans had done in 104 B.C.E.. Many architectural landmarks in the United States are essentially Roman in style, most of the federal and public service buildings are dated in Roman numerals. A type face called Roman is the most widely used in the publishing and printing industry. These are just a few examples of the continuity as we shall soon see of Afrikan High Culture being carried over into the Greco-Roman era through Britian and on to Euro-America.

Now I can imagine the idea of the Afrikan origin of science and civilization is difficult for some Black Folks to accept but it is none the less real, for my beloved Black People you surely must come to realize that everything of true value in this world was originally a product of your Afrikan genuis. It is true that things have drastically changed in the present world and we have suffered much as Rev. Sterling Means puts it "slavery is a curse to any people" but it was our Afrikan culture and a subconscious sense of our eternalness which has brought us thus far along the way. Fortunately there are some dedicated Black scholars who love this race so much they are steadfastly determined to penetrate the tangled web of ignorance which imprisons our minds and enthralls many of us in a lethargic state of racial complacency. Priceless knowledge like precious jewels lay all about us, we must wake up and reap its life giving benefits for the greatest of all riches in the world is the golden knowledge of self. Dr. Diop puts the question "Why were the Nubians and Egyptians already civilized while the rest of the world, especially all of Europe, was plunged in barbarism? That is a fact which has been observed, not the fruit of imagination. Nor is it a miraculous, inexplicable fact. Accordingly, the historian need not be astonished by it; his role ought to be that of seeking out and presenting plausible explanation for such phenomena."[77]

FROM AFRIKA TO ROME TO BRITIAN

Here again it is fitting to quote Diop "Throughout the entire Aegean epoch, the Negro influence preceded that of the Indo-European. All the population from the periphery of the Mediterranean at the time were Negroes or Negroids: Egyptians, Phoenicians; what whites there were came under the economic and cultural Egypto-Phoenician influence:. . ."[78] The superior culture of the Egypto-Phoenician society spread to the island of Crete off the coast of Greece in the Mediterranean sea around 3,000 B.C.E.. Then began the cultural dominance of the Black Minoan civilization which was in proximity to southern Europe.

In the book Man, God and Civilization Dr. John G. Jackson graphically despicts some of the splendors of this period in Crete. "The ancestors of the Cretans were natives of Afrika, a branch of the western Ethiopians,. . .The seat of these kings was a huge structure, five stories high, and spread out over an area of four acres. On the walls of its numerous rooms were beautiful frescoes and mosiacs of high artistic merit. In this palace were bathrooms with terra cotta bath tubs, fitted with drains quite modern in construction. They were made of faucet-jointed pipes superior to anything known to the later Romans and were not equalled in modern times until the mid-nineteenth century. . .Throughout Crete were attractive and comfortable homes, well-constructed ports, and fine paved roads. . . Around 1,400 B.C. this splendid culture was laid in ruins by an invasion of semi-barbarous Greeks from the north; and upon the ruins of the Cretan culture the Greeks in later days built their civilization. These Greeks were the first civilized white folks."[79]

It was not until around the 6th Century B.C.E. that the civilization of Greece entered its golden age and this was due largely to the Afrikan presence there and the decree of Pharoah Amasis which relaxed immigration restrictions against the Greeks and allowed some of them to come to Egypt and do research there.[80] This period of Greek history is marked by intellectual activity of greater diversity, vigor and grandeur than any white civilization has produced before or since and is the basis for every form of expression now common to European culture.

As the Greeks had so greatly benefitted from over 500 years of Ethiopian and Egyptian colonization and training so too did the rather thick headed militaristic Romans through some two centuries of Greek influence receive the gift of the remnants of Afrikan High Culture civilization in that area. Between 147 and 146 B.C.E. Greece became a Roman province and the learning and science of the Hellenistic age which had been created and sustained by the master teachers from Afrika, whom many of the Greeks worshipped as "gods from the land of the immortals" began to decline.[81] By 168 B.C.E. the Romans, who traced their origin back to Remus and Romulus - the children of a she-wolf, defeated the Greeks for control of the Mediterranean area.[82]

In 264 B.C.E. Rome again became embroiled in a military struggle for supremacy in the Mediterranean world, this time with a nation of Afrikans called Carthaginians. The metropolis of Carthage was founded by Phoenician colonists from the east around 814 B.C.E. under the guidance of the Black Queen Dido. Jackson says ". . .the Carthaginians and their Phoenicians forebearers were culturally and intellectually superior to the Romans. . .superior in everything relating to science. The library of Carthage is said to have contained about 500,000 volumes and these no doubt dealt with the history and the sciences of Phoenicia as a whole. . . The Phoenician seafarers and traders operated tin mines in Cornwall and swapped goods with the ancient Britons; their ships circumnavigated Afrika and crossed the Atlantic to America. . . The Phoenicians were great merchants and mariners. Not being warlike, they neglected military affairs; and this finally led to their undoing."[83] The Carthaginian general Hannibal Barca, one of the greatest military geniuses of all times, barely missed destroying Rome and it was only through the treachery of one of his own Black countrymen, King Massinissa that he was finally defeated by the Roman armies under the command of Scipio the Elder at the battle of Zama in 202 B.C.E. This defeat of Hannibal's armies ended the dominating control of the Afrikan in the Mediterranean world until the coming of the Blackamoors in the 8th Century C.E.[84] For a vivid account of the exciting exploits of Hannibal read *World's Great Men of Color*, Vol. I, p.p. 42-56.

THE ROMAN CONQUEST OF BRITAIN

In 146 B.C.E. Romans armies completely destroyed the city of Carthage making Rome the undisputed master of North Afrika and the rest of the Mediterranean sphere. She was then free to turn her legions northward with the vision of conquering the Gauls of ancient France. After defeating the Gauls Julius Caesar, then a General in the Roman Army, crossed the English Channel and landed in Britain in 55 B.C.E.. On this occasion he did some reconnaissance, made notes in his diary and returned to mainland Europe. The following year he returned with his legions and subdued the island, during this invasion Julius encountered the wild and savage Picts from Scotland who painted themselves blue in imitation, adoration and sometimes envy of the rich dark color of the many Black tribes who inhabited parts of the British Isles at the time.

According to Julius Caesar's report when he landed in Britain many of the Celti-Iberians were still residing there and the ruling tribe among them was called Silures. Tacitus, a Roman writer of the period, describes them as "swarthy (the German word for Black) with curly hair."[85] The loosely fragmented and independent tribes of Blacks and whites on the islands were collectively referred to by Julius Caesar as Britons, a term later adapted by the English as a designation for the United Kingdom of Great Britain.

Julius Caesar's *Report on the Gallic Wars*, Book V, 14, mentions that incest was still widely practiced among the Briton-Celts (whites) and that men cohabited with their mothers and had children by them "groups of ten or twelve men had wives together in common and particularly brothers along with brothers and fathers with sons."[86]

At the time of the first Roman invasion of Britain the rich tin and iron mining industries which had been established on the islands by the Afrikan-Iberians many centuries earlier and nutured by the Black Phoenician mariners were still flourishing there. After insuring the various tribes of autonomous political independence and exacting promises of tribute to the Roman treasury the bisexual Julius Caesar returned to his homeland. It was to be nearly a century before the Roman legions would invade Britain again.

HELL HATH NO FURY LIKE A WOMAN SCORNED

In 43 C.E. the Roman Emperor Claudius again initiated the conquest of Britain, crossing the English Channel with an army of 40,000, he invaded the island and was met by the Black Silures who stubbornly resisted the aggression of Rome's legionnaires for over thirty years. The Silures and the fragmented white Briton tribes were finally subdued by the year 79 C.E. and Britain became an imperial province administrated by Roman governors, this tenure lasted until the withdrawal of Roman troops in 409.

During the long period of Roman occupation the island was dubbed Britannia and Latin became the language of politics, law, literature and the educated minority (most Europeans could not read even into the 19th Century) but among the general populace the underdeveloped so-called Celtic tongue survived. The Latin language, which in its classical form was so strongly inculcated with the Punic tongue of northern Afrika, was brought to Britain by the Roman legions and so liberally impregnated the sparse language of the wild Celtic tribes that it aided tremendously in the evolvement of the hybrid bastardized English language into one of the most spoken tongues in the world today.[87] For example, "money" - that all provocative word so frequently used in the world of high and low finance is derived from the Roman designation "moneta" the name of one of the temples of the maternal goddess Juno Moneta - the Latin equivalent of the Afrikan Yemaja - where the Romans minted their coins.

In the early period of Roman occupation, during the reign of the pyromaniac Nero in the year 61 C.E., there occured between Rome's garrisons and Queen Boadicea of the Iceni tribes of eastern Britain one of the bloodiest episodes on record. This fierce revolt was occasioned by the death of Boadicea's husband King Prasutagus, at which time the Romans seized her territory, plundered her realm and sold many of the leading citizens into slavery. Boadicea was beaten and tortured and her two daughters were raped by Roman officers who treated them as common slaves. In vengeful retaliation and rage Boadicea raised a large army out of the scattered remains of the Iceni tribesmen to the strength of 200,000. Furiously plunging forward with her daughters in a horse drawn carriage, she led this undisciplined force to victory over several Roman legions.

During this violent encounter she put to death some 70,000 Romans and their allies and burned the city of London, formerly built by the Romans, to the ground. Gauis Suetonius Paulinus, then governor of the province, finally caught up with the rebel forces and overthrew them slaughtering some 80,000 Britons in a lake of blood. In despair, loathing the idea of being captured by the Romans, Boadicea took poison and died, thus cheating the Romans of a gloating victory over her person.

Eighty-eight years earlier in 27 B.C.E. the Roman armies had met with another formidable female foe, this time in the person of the Black Queen Candace of Ethiopia. Concerning this wonderful event Diop writes "When the Indo-European world acquired enough military strength to conquer the old countries that had civilized it, they encountered the fierce, unyielding resistance of a queen whose determined struggle symbolized the national pride of a people who, until then, had commanded others. This was Queen Candace of the Meroitic Sudan. She impressed all antiquity by her stand at the head of her troops against the Roman armies of Augustus Caesar. The loss of an eye in battle only redoubled her courage; her fearlessness and scorn of death even forced the admiration of a chauvinist like Strabo. . ."[88] At the head of her army she so ferociously opposed the iron fisted might of the Roman army that even though the latter won in the military struggle their soldiers were weary and so battered that Rome never had a mind to engage in conflict with Ethiopia again. As the old saying goes "they knew they had been in a sho nuff fight."

The source of the conflict started when the Roman senate in a frantic search for new sources of revenue had the audacity to attempt a burden of tribute (that is taxation) on the Ethiopian kingdom of Meroe. These proud Afrikans who descended from the oldest line of rulers in the world, courageous and magnificent in their self-determination rose up in arms under the brave and heroic leadership of Queen Candace and even though they lacked the superior weapons technology of the Roman army they put up such a heroic fight that the loss in lives and resources to the Roman empire was horrendous. The Roman senate then decided it would be more to their advantage to dispense with the issue as quitely as possible. Whereupon an overwhelming majority voted to rescend the tribute and Augustus ordered the evacuation of his troops from the Sudan, in the Land of the Blacks. When the queen's delegation met with representatives of the Roman government Caesar Augustus met their demands to the complete satisfaction of the Ethiopian people.[89]

Some nineteen centuries later, 1886 and 1941 successively, Rome in the person of the Italian government seeking to expand the sphere of its colonial holdings set out to invade Ethiopia once again. In 1896 the Italians were bitterly defeated and driven out of the eternal land by strong willed Ethiopian fighting forces under the masterful leadership of one of Candace's direct descendants, Menelik II.[90] It was not until the dictatorship of Benito Mussolini, a partner of Adolph Hitler, that Italy made good her ambition and conquered this most ancient Afrikan kingdom in the mid-1930's. During this conflict many a Black man, blessed with the divine gift of the true knowledge of self, who resided in the United States and other parts of the world answered the call to arms and went to fight side by side with their Ethiopian brothers, one of the most outstanding of these Afrikan patriots was Julian Richardson, the fabulous "Black Eagle". Eventually in 1945 Haile Selassie, Candace's great-grandchild nineteen centuries removed, returned to his beloved country and headed a force of 250,000 Blacks which drove the Italians into the Red Sea, thus liberating that portion of Ethiopia's Eternal Motherland.[91]

BROTHERS IN BARBARITY

About the time of the first Roman conquest of Britain Cicero the unofficial leader of the senate wrote a friend advising him not to buy British slaves because they had "no men of letters or any fine hand in music. . .could not be taught and were. . .the stupidest and ugliest slaves in the world."[92] Other Roman writers of the period also reported much about the barbarity of the Picts and white-Celts of Britannia, who fought in the nude and painted themselves blue and other colors.[93] Yet the awful practice of infanticide was still being commonly practiced in the imperial city of Rome. This custom of leaving baby girls abandoned in baskets to die of exposure, starvation or other chance happenings continued in Rome up until the fourth century. One of the provisions of Rome's most ancient law, called the "laws of Romulus", was for parents to raise all male children and the first born female, all other unwanted infant girls were to be abandoned.[94] This seems to have been a very widespread custom all over Europe and in some parts of Asia.

Around 115 the wild and barbarous Picts of Caledonia (today's Scotland) annihilated all the inhabitants of a Roman fortress in consequence of which the Roman emperor Hadrian in 122 ordered the construction of a 73 mile long wall, 20 feet high and 8 feet thick which stretched east to west from coast to coast. This prohibiting structure deterred future invasions of Britannia by Scotlands recalcitrant tribes and for a time brought peace in the province.

A BLACK EMPEROR RESTORES LAW
AND ORDER IN BRITAIN

After his brilliant victories over Clodius Albinus, his white rival for the imperial throne and the savage German tribes of Gaul, the Afrikan Septimius Severus supported by his legions in the year 193 C.E. became Roman emperor (which is tantamount to a Black Man becoming president of the United States). In 197 Severus mercilessly subdues rebellions in Gaul and Britain. When he first entered Britannia at the head of his troops he was welcomed and hailed by the general populace as a messianic deliverer from the Gauls and Germans who continually ravaged and pillaged the islands. Emperor Severus drove the aliens back across the English Channel into mainland Europe and established what came to be known as a century of peace for there were no more attempted invasions from the north for over a hundred years.[95]

Septimius Serverus was born April 11, 146 C.E. in Numidia, Afrika, the product of an upper middle class Black family, he received a liberal education in Latin, which he spoke with an Afrikan accent all the days of his life, juris prudence, military science and astrology.[96] Though he grew to appreciate Latin literature and eventually became the emperor of Rome, an essentially white nation, he himself maintained his basic Afrikan culture even unto his eating habits for he gave strict orders for special foodstuffs to be transported from Afrika to Europe in order to supply his table with an abundance of soul cuisine.[97] Most of Septimius Serverus' top officials were Afrikans, he also conferred the semi-autonomous status of "home rule" (that is an independent commonwealth province within the imperial Roman structure) on his homeland in Afrika and ordered the remains of his fellow Afrikan soul brother, Hannibal Barca" to be interred in a marble and gold monument which he erected in the midst of the Roman square.[98]

Around 202 Septimius visited Egypt where he appears to have done some investigative research into the Ancient Mysteries of the Nile Valley higher learning centers - for it is recorded that his probing intellectual curiosity left nothing uninvestigated.[99] From there he returned to Rome in triumph at which time an arch was built which still bears his name in commemoration of this great event. In 208 he again went to Britain to supervise the upgrading of mechanical defense systems and refurbish the Hadrian Wall. On February 4, 211, while at York, England, Emperor Septimius Serverus died of pneumonia at the age of sixty-four and passed on to the glorious realm of his Afrikan Ancestors. There were many other Afrikan emperors of the Roman empire which space does not permit us to expound upon in this book but for a partial list of these great Black leaders of the Latin world see *Profiles in Afrikan Heritage* by Edward L. Jones.[100]

THE END OF ROMAN OCCUPATION
BRINGS THE DARK AGES TO EUROPE

During the reign of another Black emperor of the Roman empire, Flavius Honorius who came to the throne in 395, uncivilized German tribes known as Goths escalated their invasion of the western half of the Roman domain. In 409 most of the Roman legions withdrew from Britain to fight the Goths in Italy, when the city of Rome was sacked in 410 the last imperial forces were recalled from the island and shortly after the death of Honorius in 423 wild Germanic tribes overran Gaul and the former Roman province of Britannia. White-Celtic culture again became dominate and Latin civilization in Britain quickly disintergrated. The Latin conquest of Gaul and Britain laid the foundation upon which the later development of European society was built yet it would be centuries before this process was complete, for after the withdrawal of the Roman forces from the northwestern sector of Europe the continent plunged into the political chaos, intellectual stagnation and ignorance of medieval times commonly known as the Dark Ages. The Dark Ages extended over a period of more than a thousand years marked by incessant war and strife.

During their occupation of Britain the Romans had brought with them to western Europe the concept of bath houses which they had received from the Phoenicians and the Greeks. After their departure, the Britons, Gauls, and Germanics returned to the squalor of their former ways. [101]   At the decline of the Roman empire all of western Europe was overrun by plundering hordes of Germanic tribes from the far north such as the Ostrogoths, Visigoths, Saxons, Jutes and most notably the ultra-destructive Vandals who invaded north Afrika in 429 C.E.. Concerning the activities of this group John G. Jackson writes "the Vandals established a tyranny in that region that was destructive in the highest degree. . .They found Africa flourishing and they left it desolate, with its great buildings thrown down, its people reduced to slavery and the Church of Africa, so important in the early days of Christianity, practically non-existant." [102]   Yet out of this same region which had suffered so greatly from the rampant destructive vandalism of Germanic overlords was, a few centuries later, to emerge the new Black civilizers of Europe, the Moors. In the 8th Century the Blackamoors conquered Spain, Portugal, southern France, parts of Italy and as late as the Tenth Century these Afrikan rulers held supreme sovereignty over three provinces in Scotland. [103]

Chapter Five

Britain During The Dark Ages

CHAPTER FIVE

BRITAIN DURING THE DARK AGES

THE GERMANIC INVASIONS

At the end of the Roman occupation of Britain seafaring Germanic tribes including the Angles, Saxons, and Jutes, continued to carry on many raids along the coastal regions of the island. About 425 C.E. when Germanic war bands crossed the North Sea from the low countries (land of the Nordics) of Europe they penetrated Ireland and burned to the ground those institutions of learning which had once been enriched by the Celti-Iberian culture of the Blacks who from the dawn of history had been the dominate population there. At this time the white populace became English slaves for over 700 years, the Blacks were mostly exterminated and sold into slavery in other lands.

Jutes were probably the first to land on the island around 449, they settled in the southeast corner of Britain. Other German tribes followed, setting up tribal kingdoms throughout the southern and eastern portion of the island. The area conquered by the Angles was called Anglaland, or Englaland from which came England. As the Germanic tribes swept into England, they gradually pushed the Britons further and further west into the territory of the Blacks there. The few remaining Black tribes descendant from the ancient Iberians moved north to Scotland and west to the hill country of Wales. The Britons held out for a number of years against the Teutons under the leadership of a strong king, this may have been the legendary King Arthur of Camelot fame. The designation German comes from the Latin "germanus" meaning "closely related." The Romans used this terminology in a derogatory manner in reference to the pathological sense of the word germ denoting the germy unkept appearance, filthy hovels and lifestyles of the European tribes to the north.

Around 449 a British tribal chieftain named Vortigern invited the Germans to come to Britain and help him fight off the invading Picts from Scotland, but a quarrel soon broke out between the Britons and their allies and the Germans began to drive the Britons off the land. By the end of the Fourth Century the Angles, Saxons and Jutes occupied nearly all of England to the borders of Scotland in the north and the borders of Wales in the west. In the two centuries from Augustus (27 B.C.E. - 14 C.E.) to Aurelius (161 - 180 C.E.) the Germans passed from an exclusively migratory life of hunting and herding to one of agriculture and village life but they were still so inculcated with nomad fever that they rapidly exhausted the land and then moved on to conquer new acreage by the sword. Basic to the German nature was violence and war was his "meat and drink", the Roman writer Tacitus says "to cultivate the earth and wait the regular produce of the seasons is not the maxims of a German; you will more rapidly persuade him to attack the enemy and provoke honorable wounds on the field of battle. To earn by the sweat of your brow what you might gain at the price of your blood is in the opinion of a German a sluggish principle, unworthy of a soldier."[104] This attitude towards agriculture on the part of the Germans demonstrates another great difference between the early whites and ancient peoples of color who generally lived in sedentary and agrarian societies. Agrarian life is the basis of all civilization and culture. The word "culture" is itself rooted in the tilling of the soil and a component of the term "agriculture". The farther you stray from the land the farther you drift away from the semblance of any real civilization.

When not engaged in some violent activity the men of the Germanic tribes were basically lazy. If not occupied with some form of bloodletting they passed the time away gambling while eating gluttonous meals of near raw flesh and drinking rivers of beer. In the German matrimonial system the groom literally bought his wife from her father using cattle or weapons as the medium of exchange. In their society each man had the power of life and death over his wife and children, he could sell or destroy them whenever it suited his fancy to do so.[106] According to Rogers, during this period of English history cannibalism (that is the eaing of human flesh) was openly practiced at the court of King Ethelfrith.[106] In all fairness we must admit that cannibalism did exist among some Asian and Afrikan tribes who were forced by natural catastrophe and Euro-Asian slave hunting excursions to live under extremely harsh conditions.[107] But the practice of eating people was far more widely spread among the Indo-European Caucasians even into his so-called high society, especially in the case of the ancestors of the new staunchy British who flaunt themselves as being the most civilized and superior people in the world.

In modern times the Anglo-Saxon, Euro-American nation of the United States still pay homage to the dieties of their German ancestors four days out of every week, i.e. Tuesday - named so after the German god Tiu a Norse diety of war, the son of Wodin (Odin).

Wednesday in honor of "Wodin" the chief war god in Teutonic mythology unto whom was offered the smelly sacrifice of human victims. Thursday in homage to "Thor" the German god of thunder and Friday after "Frigg" or "Freya" the Norse goddess of love and springtime.

LATIN - A MAGIC LANGUAGE

A very small minority of Hitler's ancestors, the Germans, could read and write, their literary achievement, if it can really be called such, consisted of adaptation of certain characters of the Latin alphabet to make up a German system called the "runes", a Gothic word meaning "secret". The runes were associated with mystery and secrecy because they were used in the magic formulas of witchcraft practices and demonology ceremonies. So only a very few persons knew them, otherwise nearly all of the populace was illiterate. Meanwhile, in sharp contrast to the Germans in western Europe, the Phoenician, Egyptian, Ethiopian, Iberian and the Mediterranean offspring cultures of the Greeks and Romans were still flourishing in the East.

For centruies Latin was considered by the Germans and other Europeans to be a magic language. Thus in this way did Roman civilization survive the collapse of the empire and become a common European possession. The Latin language, which in its vulgar form gave birth to all the so-called romance languages such as Italian, French, Portuguese, Spanish, etc. and in its literary form survived until the Seventeenth Century as the common intellectual tongue of Europe's few learned men. All books were written in Latin and it became the international language of intercontinental commerce. This language which had been preserved by the Black Saint Tertullian became the official language of the Roman Catholic Church.[108]

EUROPEAN CHRISTIANITY VERSUS
THE AFRIKAN MYSTERY SCHOOLS

It was under the auspices of the Roman empire that the so-called Christian religion - supposedly based on the life and death of an Afrikan named Jesus ben Joseph called the Christ who was born in Palestine - penetrated Europe in the Fourth Century.[109] A very large majority of the population, mainly the peasants, remained unaffected by it. The turning point came in 312 C.E. when Emperor Constantine declared himself a Christian and the mass of his subjects began following his example, at first some voluntarily, and later by

43

his imperial command. Before the end of the Fourth Century Christianity had, by force of arms, become obligatory and all other forms of belief and worship were forbidden. The Roman Catholic priesthood then became an official body and from that point on formed a vital part of the European aristocracy. In 325 C.E. Constantine commanded 310 bishops of Europe and Asia Minor to convene at the Nicean Council in Turkey. At this council the co-optation of the Afrikan church, the original church, was completed and the future doctrine of the Roman Catholic Church was firmly established by the might of the Roman army.

In 529 Emperor Justinian I again through the power of military force ordered the closing of all the Mystery Schools founded by the Ancient Afrikan High Culture System which had spread to Europe from Egypt. At the time Afrika was regarded as the holy land by most peoples of the ancient world. This high regard for the Blacks and their lofty High Culture learning systems filled Rome with envy, consequently she legalized Christianity, which she had previously persecuted for over three long centuries and set it up as the state religion. Thus the remains of the Roman empire pitted Christianity against its own mother the High Culture Systems of the Afrikan Mystery Schools. [110]

EUROPEAN CHRISTIANITY
A CONTINUATION OF THE ROMAN EMPIRE

During Europe's dark ages (410 - 1798) Roman Christianity became an extension of the declining Roman empire and opened to northern Europe the gateway to the eastern civilization of the Byzantine empire (395-1453). The only tie that bound all western Europe together in a quasi-political and ecclesiastical unity was the Catholic Church centering in the Pope at the Vatican in Rome. The Roman papacy eventually grew so strong that it controlled all the rulers of Europe and imposed upon these princes the duty of exterminating all heretics (non-adherents to official Catholic Doctrine) and the obligation of confession to the clergy. This uniform system of repression, supervision and preaching was established in every country in Europe, thus European ideological and political unity was set up under the absolute and very seldom contested authority of the Pope of Rome. At first European Christianity, which is an extension of Judo-Greco-Latin culture in its turn a by product of the Egyptian Mystery System, had somewhat of a restraining effect on Europe. It was either Christianity or utter barbarity for that continent, although at times one could hardly tell the difference between the two.

The Christianity of the Afrikan Church, the original church, founded by Black bishops such as Cyprian, Origen, Turtellian, Augustine and other Afrikan devotees, asserted the dominate civilizing influence in Europe until with the aid of the emperor's armies it was totally co-opted by the Roman Popes. But even this corrupted version of an age old doctrine kept Europe from utterly regressing into a Neanderthal state.

AUSTIN - THE UNWILLING MISSIONARY: THE MAN WHO DIDN'T WANT TO GO

In 596 Pope Gregory I endeavoring to spread his spiritual dominion over distant lands commissioned Augustine (named after the Afrikan St. Augustine (354 - 430 C.E.) and forty other Benedictine monks to go from Rome to England as missionaries and convert the wild Germanic tribes to Christianity. When Augustine, who was also called Austin, and his company reached France they were overwhelmingly terrified by the reports of the savage inhabitants of the British Isles, whereupon Austin aborted his mission, returned to Rome and in suppliant humility begged the Pope to be merciful and release him from his assignment but Gregory would not hear of it and made him go to Britain anyway. Fortunately for Austin and his party, upon landing on the isle, they were welcomed by Bertha, the wife of King Ethelbert, who herself had been sprinkled a Christian. Encouraged by this warm reception Austin commenced his work of six years during which time he founded and became the first Archbishop of Canterbury which became the headquarters of the Britain's ecclesiastical domain, thus did Austin institute the European Christian Church in England. On June 2, 597 Austin converted King Ethelbert of the Jutes who controlled the southern portion of England and baptized (sprinkled) him into the Roman Catholic Church.

Austin was a member of the Benedictine monastic order and it was this religious fraternity which kept alive and disseminated any degree of culture and learning in Britain and mainland Europe during the Dark Ages, until the coming of the Moors. One of the main handicaps of monastic life and European Christians in general is they seldom bathed, in fact to some European Christian organizations it was considered a sin to bathe. The cleanliness question was one of the primary bones of contention the Europeans had with the Afrikan Mystery System of which bathing was a constant ritual.[111] This aversion which Europeans had to water is no doubt the reason why the Roman Catholic's adopted sprinkle baptism instead of the original procedure of total submersion. The sharing of this information is not an attempt to attack anyone's religious denominational preference but a statement of historical fact.

During this period the Byzantine Empire, ever in constant contact with the civilizing hand of the east, preserved important elements of Greco-Roman learning throughout the middle ages. Otherwise respect for learning on the European continent, outside of Moorish Spain, was perpetuated mainly in certain of the monastic orders, however the clergy themselves were little interested in theological study or classical learning. Most of the books produced at the time were then written with no other view than to deceive the simple-minded multitudes who at that time formed the great bulk of the European community. According to the booklet *Crimes of Christianity* "no fable could be too gross, no invention too transparent, for their unsuspicious acceptance, if it assumed a pious form or tended to edification." No period of the history of the world ever produced so many forged works as the first few centuries of the Christian era.

During this age scientific investigation consisted of such "serious" problems as; how many celestrial angels could sit on the head of a stick pin. Pieces of flesh said to be the foreskin of the penis of Jesus Christ along with shiploads of splinters from his cross were sold by the clergy to the ignorant masses at exorbitant prices. The blood of Christ, his hair and his teeth and bottles upon bottles of milk on which he was supposed to have been suckled were exhibited in over a hundred places throughout Europe for the adoration of the paying devotees of the Roman Catholic Church.[112]   By the Eighth Century education had fallen so low that the clergy themselves, the sole guardians of the Roman culture, could write nothing but a kind of barbarous Latin in an almost illegible script.

AND THEN CAME THE MOORS

In 711 C.E. an Afrikan People known as the Moors under the leader Gebel Tarik crossed the straits, landed on the rock island of Gibralter, (named in his honor) and here built a mighty fortress. From this base of operations they entered Europe, defeated the German Goths and made themselves masters of Spain. Then the Moors crossed the Pyrenees Mountains and conquered southern France giving all this backward region one of the finest cultures Europe has ever had.[113]   This great Muslim empire included more land than did the Roman empire in its heyday. These Blacks brought with them to Spain a culture far exceeding that possessed by any of the European people of the time.

Black Muslim scholars who introduced into Europe the system of Arabic numerals which included the zero were masters of astronomy, mathematics, medicine, chemistry and physics and possessed a vigorous knowledge of the classics. These wise and brilliant scholars founded great universities in Spain and initiated a golden age of learning and culture which slowly but surely eventually diffused throughout western Europe.[114] Before the coming of the Blackamoors there was no such thing as the concept of chivalry of stately court life among the European aristocracy.[115] Rogers says "that while the Moorish kings of Spain were living in magnificent palaces the kings of England, France and Germany had homes little better than stables - chimneyless, windowless and with a hole in the roof for the smoke to escape."[116]

Around the year 770 B.C.E. a Black general by the name of Douglas whose name means "behold the Black or swarthy-colored man" was racking up victories through his magnificent military exploits in Scotland.[117] This was Britain and Europe in general during the period of the dark ages.

Chapter Six

The Foundations of White Anglo-Saxon Britain

CHAPTER SIX

THE FOUNDATIONS OF WHITE ANGLO-SAXON BRITAIN

AFRIKAN ORIGIN OF THE SAXONS

Anglo-Saxon is the name given a Caucasian group created by the union of two Germanic tribes that settled in England between the Fifth and Ninth Centuries C.E.. Oddly enough Godfrey Higgins says the term Saxon comes from the word "Saca" or "Sacya" sometimes called "Shaka". This name and its variations was one of the universal designations of the Black Buddha (enlightened one) which gives evidence to the fact that the original people who brought live and settlement to the regions, later encroached upon and claimed during the migrations of the Germanic tribes, were Black men from India. Higgins also states that the philosophy of the Black Buddhas which he calls the religion of the Om (the One, the Unmoved Mover) was at one time circulated all over the Earth. Again he says the word "Saca" means "using the mind" or "to contemplate wisdom".[118] This fact again confirms the reality that there is not a corner of the globe where the Black Man has not traveled and left much to corroborate his having touched it with the divine light of Amen-Ra, that is the High Culture Systems of Ancient Ethiopia and Egypt. Much of this evidence is subtly hidden in the mythology of all European cultures, that is why whites have this great need to claim the ancient high civilizations of India and Egypt as their own. The great need on the part of the whites to create for themselves a pseudo-culture also provides the impetus for their many secret societies, such as the Masons, Rosicrucians, Illuminate etc..

Further demonstrations of the inherent inferiority complex of Caucasians in the face of the overwhelming majority world of color is made manifest in the tendency of the European towards the domination of non-whites. [119]   At every turn, whenever possible, as is so well documented by the panorama of history, Europeans subdue Blacks and other peoples of color, co-opt their culture and hide from them and the future generations of their posterity the material and esoteric sciences which were originally bequeathed unto them by age old civilizatiions. This activity on the part of the Caucasian is motivated by his great fear of the Afrikan for he well understands that once the Black man, as foretold by the Honorable Marcus Garvey, the Honorable Elijah Muhammad and many others is resurrected from mental death and embraces the high sciences of his true self the days of European domination will be in the last ten digits of the countdown to a new world order wherein by reason of his historical phenomenon the white man has no place. Oh! What fools these descendants of the original cavemen are, it would have been better for them to have made a sincere and honest peace with us who were and will again become the rightful rulers of the Earth. No matter what they have done or what they now do they cannot stop an idea whose time has come. The Creator's Master Plan for the Black Man will surely be realized and fulfilled in all of its wonder and magnificence, in those days the words of the old Black Spiritual will come to life with new meaning "Satan, we gonna bring your kingdom down."

The original mystic knowledge of the Black Man co-opted by the barbarous German tribes which later became known as Saxons was taken in part by them and degenerated into rituals of human sacrifice and cannibalism. Here is another case of how the divine light of the Afrikan was misappropiated by demon-ridden Europeans and depreciated into a dim shadow of its former glory. The Anglo-Saxon dominated societies in the world today such as the United States of America, England, etc., for all their technological advances are still merely smouldering embers of the hidden High Culture of the Original Black Man. [120]

When the nomadic German tribe, who later confiscated and adopted the name Saxon, was driven out of the lands in northeastern Europe in which they had loosely settled they passed through other lands inhabited by immigrant tribes in search of new habitations. This migration continued westward until the wandering tribes reached the seacoast and could go no further and when the Germanic tribes sought to seize the land from the indigenous inhabitants a desperate struggle took place, the brutal warlike nature of the Germans prevailed and this is how the Anglo-Saxon took possession of Britain.

THE UNITED STATES OF AMERICA AND ANGLO-SAXON CULTURE

Today's Euro-American ruling class known as the WASP's (White Anglo-Saxon Protestants), like their European ancestors of old, still have a sensual ecstasy for violence. The Americans blissful preoccupation with violence is well exhibited in the "beat freakism" plots of the most popular movie and television shows and the "kinky sex" of their cocaine snorting so-called high society. We are taking

49

the time to recount these key factors of Anglo-Saxon culture at this point because it is the foundation of which the mores and lifestyles of all the later English speaking colonizers including the United States of America is built. We do this also to set forth another prime example of the distinct personality and worldview of the Euro-American which is in great contrast to the outlook of most of the Black descendants of the Afrikans who were captured from their native land and sold into bondage on these shores. It is because of this age old contrast that we as a people have such difficulty communicating with whites on the basis of justice and righteousness. What Black People, residing in this country or any other white dominated land, must clearly and pragmatically come to understand is that regardless to the lofty ideals engraved on paper in such documents as the United States Constitution, the Declaration of Independence, etc., the basic Anglo-Saxon nature of the Euro-American white man remains virtually unchanged. A close study and scrutinization of this factor and the use of intelligent logic instead of emotionalized sentimentality will help us to understand clearly that the mere expression of lofty ideals does not change the nature of a people for if it did Black People would essentially have no problem of justice and equal rights in America today. Think of that.

The English language, once considered to be vulgar and profane speech by the aristocracy of Europe, is the official language of the United States. English is rooted in the Anglo-Saxon tongues which according to Higgins is a remnant of the original tongues taught to the ancient Saxons by the Blacks and bears traces of the Ethiopian language left behind by the Iberians who first inhabited the British Isles. [121] There are still many Hebrew, Indian, Arabic and Ethiopian words used in the language today. As a matter of fact during the American Revolution there was a popular proposal to replace English with Hebrew as the official language of the United States. Hebrew was believed by the colonists to be the mother of all tongues and until 1817 the annual commencement addresses at Harvard were delivered in Hebrew. [122]

THE CRUDE ANGLO-SAXON LIFESTYLE

Anglo-Saxon economy like its law was primitive and far less developed than Roman Britian. The Anglo-Saxons loved to indulge in heavy feasting signally the consumption of flesh and very hard drinking. In their society wives and children could be sold into slavery by husbands or fathers in need. Owners of slaves were at liberty to kill them at will. Even in those days of Ninth Century England the main commerce of the seaport town of Bristol was the trafficking of slaves which at that time was brought in from the neighboring land of Ireland. Education like everything else suffered as a result of the Germanic invasions.

After the Anglo-Saxon homogeneity England slowly began to recover intellectually due in part to the conversion of the Anglo-Saxon kings of Christianity, which was the direct result of the labors of the remaining Black Celti-Iberians scholars and Roman Catholic missionaries. This strange and abnormal coalition of a centuries old rivalry founded the schools and libraries which eventually made England one of the leaders of European learning north of the Alps from the Ninth Century on. The Roman Church, a direct offshoot of the earliest Christian Church - the Afrikan Church, for all its stagnation and perpetuation of ignorance among the masses - who in most parts of Europe were forbidden to read any book including the Bible oft times upon pain of death - played a very decisive role in the making of English civilization. The other chief element being the advanced culture of the Afrikan in the person of the Moors who were bringing the Higher Culture and enlightenment of their civilization to southern Europe.

THE INVASION OF THE VIKINGS

DANISH VIKINGS

In the year 787 Danish Vikings described by Catholic monks as "wild and letterless pagans" invaded England, slaughtered many of the civilian populace, sacked the monestaries, - the only centers of learning in the area - destroyed and scattered existing libraries, and reduced most of the schools to destitution. By 877 the Danes held large portions of eastern and central England. Culturally the Danish invasion was a blight. The Anglo-Saxon culture founded for them by the Celti-Iberians and the Latin Church was all but demolished. Architecture marked time, illumination and art decayed and intellectual progress was checked and held in limbo for over two centuries. About this time there appeared on the scene one Egbert, the Saxon king of Wessex, who began to unify the various Anglo-Saxon kingdoms and by the end of his reign in 836 all the other kings recognized his supremacy. Thus Egbert became the first king of England.

In 871 Albert called the Great came to the throne and reigned until 899. In 878 Alfred forced the Danes to agree to stay within the area east of the island called Danelaw. King Alfred, who suffered periodically from epiliptic fits, had the benefits of traveling to other parts of the world outside of England, this experience brought home to him the backward condition of his homeland. During his reign he undertook the awesome task of trying to revive culture and learning in the area.

In 1002 King Ethelred, who had previously adopted a policy of buying off the Viking invaders, massacred the Danes living in England. Among them was the sister of King Sweyn of Denmark, in vengeful retaliation King Sweyn and his son Canute again invaded England in 1013 and set Ethelred to flight. In 1016 Canute became the first of three Danish kings who were to rule all England until 1042. The church officials said he was the first civilized Viking king to come to the island. During his reign he divided England into military districts called earldoms, each ruled by an earl, hence the designation "earl of this" and "earl of that" in reference to certain members of the so-called English nobility.

It was during this period of Danish rule (around 1040) that the legendary Lady Godiva at the behest of her husband, the Earl of Mercia, rode buck naked through the streets of Coventry, England to protest the burden of heavy taxation on its citizenry. In preparation for this demonstration the Countess decreed that all the residents of Coventry should for the duration of this graphic protest keep themselves off the streets, behind locked doors and closed shutters. So the story goes, as Godiva, divested of every stitch of clothing, rode horseback through the streets of the town wearing nothing but a smile everyone strictly obeyed this decree with the exception of one Tom Taylor who sneaked a peek through a window thus giving birth to the phrase "Peeping Tom". The protest was successful and the tax was abolished.

After the brief two year reign of Canute's son Hardicanute (1040-1042) which was noted for its extreme cruelty and corruption, Edward the Confessor, dubbed such because of his devotion to Roman Catholicism, backed by the military might of Godwin the Earl of Wessex was placed on the throne of England. This action restored Saxon rule for another twenty-four years. Edward was a weak ruler, more a monk than a king, who busied himself with founding Westminster Abbey (the National Church of England where its monarchs are crowned) and left the running of the government mainly to his benefactor the Earl of Wessex. Edward died in 1066 and was proclaimed a so-called Saint by Pope Alexander III in 1161.

The Danish conquest of England was a part of that continued and long process of foreign invasions which eventually caused the population of the Bristish Isles to change from predominantly Black to virtually all white. Concerning the dominance of the Blacks in Scotland who were still there at the time of the Saxon kings in England J.A. Rogers writes "so late as the Tenth Century three of these provinces were wholly Black and the supreme ruler of these became for a time the paramount king of Scotland. . ." History knows this brother as Kenneth the Niger also called the "Dubh" meaning the "Black Man." [123] According to Rufus Harley it was the Blacks who brought the fashion of wearing kilts and the playing of bagpipes to Scotland. [124]

The Ninth and Tenth Centuries were one of the greatest periods of Moorish cultural development in southwestern Europe. These Afrikans continued to establish great libraries and universities and their distinct architecture and art which brought together elements of the east and west while at the same time permitting religious freedom to all under their domain. Before the end of the Tenth Century the Moors overran Sicily in the southern portion of the Italian Peninsula and established their High Civilization there.. [12,5] During the period of Danish rule England had become the backwater of European learning. It was to this period of revitalized Black culture in Spain, France and Italy that the English church, the center of Britain's culture and learning once again became indebted during its long upward climb towards the establishment of arts and letters.

WILLIAM THE CONQUEROR
AND THE NORMAN INVASION

Early in the Tenth Century Norsemen subjugated parts of northern France and formed the kingdom of Normandy, its rulers soon became more powerful than the king of France. The term "Norman" means "northmen" and was applied to the roving and plundering bands of Vikings from Scandinavia. In 911, Charles III, king of western France formed a treaty with the Normans and persuaded them to retire from constant bloodshed and warfare. After paying a tribute of much gold and marrying his daughter to Rollo their leader the treaty was ratified. Rollo's most famous descendant was William the Conqueror, Duke of Normandy, cousin to Edward the Confessor. Described as a vain and ruthless ruler he entered England with an army of about 15,000 men and defeated Harold II the last Anglo-Saxon king of England.

Before carrying out his ambition to conquer England William sent envoys to consult with Alexander II, the Pope of Rome who excommunicated Harold and his supporters from the Roman

Catholic Church, condemning them to eternal damnation. The Pope then declared William of Normandy the lawful successor to the throne of England. Alexander now placed his blessing on the Duke's planned invasion by proclaiming the Norman invasion of England a "holy war". He then sent William a consecrated ring which had been kissed by the prelate's very own lips and supposedly contained a diamond with a hair from St. Peter's head in it.

In September of 1066 William the Conqueror sailed from Normandy, France with 1,400 vessels across the English Channel. On October 14th Harold II met William's army on Senlac Hill at the Battle of Hastings which was fought for nine hours. Harold, his eye pierced by an arrow and hanging halfway out of its socket, stumbled about having been blinded by the blood in his other eye and fell to the ground whereupon he was immediately butchered by Norman knights, one cut off his head, another his leg and others scattered Harold's intestines and bowels all over the field of battle. When the English troops saw this they fled in horror with the Normans in hot pursuit hacking away as they went through the broken ranks of English soldiers. So thorough was the dismembering of Harold II and the chaotic slaughter of the day that the Catholic Monks who were commissioned to find Harold's body had to go to a woman named Edith who had been his former mistress for help in identifying the parts of her fallen lover's body. On Christmas Day, 1066 William the Conqueror was crowned king of England.

When William the Conqueror invaded England he brought with him so-called Jewish moneylenders who controlled most of the money in Europe at that time, to provide a new stimulus to English trade and industry. Upon his ascension to the throne William divided the land among his Norman knights and most of the Anglo-Saxons became serfs bound to the land. But in spite of this enslavement the Anglo-Saxons kept their language and many of their customs. That is why the English language often has two words meaning the same thing, a Norman one and an Anglo-Saxon one wherein most other languages have one. The term serf comes from the Latin word "servus" which means "slaves", the status of a serf was midway between that of a free man and a slave. A serf's holdings usually included a house, the adjoining plot of land, a share of surrounding field, and a few animals. Part of his crop harvest went to the master of the manor as a rent payment. In addition the serf worked on the overlord's land and made special payments to him. During the reign of William I, England became the most centralized state in Europe during the middle ages. With an iron fist he reduced an entire kingdom to obedience, had the land divided between his leading followers, made them swear alligence to him as his direct vassals, firmly forbid the fighting of private wars and then placed all his subjects under the control of his officers, thus inaugurating the feudal system in England.

It was at this time that the Normans instituted the building of stone castles as a means of defense against a hostile Saxon population. During this period the legendary but historically obscure Robin Hood is said to have been an unbeaten rebel who lived in Sherwood Forest and provided the inspiration and leadership of a guerrilla band which for over a century carried on a struggle of resistance against their Norman overlords. Robin Hood and his band of merry men is reportedly to have robbed the rich, the Normans, and given to the poor, the Saxons. His father's land was taken from him by the king and given to someone else, that's why Robin Hood went on a robbing rampage.

In the later years of his reign, William the Conqueror became so obese that he could hardly mount a horse. At his death in 1087 his body proved to be too big for the coffin and as the funeral attendants tried to force his enormous bulk into the narrow space the body burst, filling the church with an awful stench as bowels and entrails shot forth amid the lamenting mourners in the congregation. In 1066 when William I conquered England the population was estimated at about 2,500,000. At this same time while backward England was caught in the throes of internal strife, in Afrika King Tunkamenon was reigning over the enlightened empire of Ouagadou (Ghana) with the power to put a mighty army of 200,000 well disciplined soldiers in the field. Many historians have wondered what might have been the outcome had the Normans in lieu of conquering England tried to invade Ghana instead. One must admit the thought is indeed a delightful one to those of us who are descendants of Afrikan slaves who were captured and brought to this land as a result of the British colonial expansion.

KNIGHTS, CASTLES AND FEUDALISM

Feudalism became the chief way of life on the European continent during the middle ages, Barons, Dukes, Earls and other members of the aristocracy owned most of the land and controlled the lives of the people. The Roman Catholic Church also owned much land and its ecclesiastical influence played a major part in keeping the masses of the population in serfdom. The feudal system brought to England by William the Conqueror was based upon the division of the country into very large estates held by warrior chiefs who maintained bands of mounted and armored soldiers called knights. These war chiefs and land barons in turn pledged themselves as vassals to the king whom they theoretically regarded as the ultimate owner of the land and its inhabitants, which were ever to be at his beck and call. These huge estates called fiefs became hereditary and was passed from one generation to the other, thus forever weilding the gap between the rich and the poor. This concept of personal land ownership so peculiar to the European was alien to the Afrikan and other peoples of color who held the land in common for the collective good of the people, for they reasoned; how can anyone own the earth, the sky and the air. It is the gift of God which has been perserved for us through our ancestors.

During the feudalist era of 11th and 12th century Europe, the whole countryside of England became covered with fortifications and castles and war again became the normal state of things. Kings, nobles and knights, in order to be ever ready to do battle kept their horses in the same rooms in which they slept with their wives.[126] The primary role of the knights was to police the countryside to constrain bandits, raiders, plunderers, and invaders but in many cases these same knights fell upon and exploited the unshielded masses they were pledged to protect. Masters of castles often became the terrors of the country and that which started out as a protection for the people became its most repressive force. The poor working class who lived and depended on the manors were called "villians", from which comes the word "village", because of their menial existence.[127] The strongly fortified residences, such as was occupied by European nobility in the middle ages, known as the castles developed in western Europe during the tenth century and played a very important part in the growth of the feudal system.

Because of the fantasies created by hollywood motion pictures, story books and other media imagery, a sort of glamour surrounds the idea of castle life. But in reality, a castle was a comfortless place. The interior was dark, damp, drafty and poorly ventilated. The furniture was crude and soldiers and servants alike often slept on the malodorous floors of straw. Castle life was desirable only in contrast to living in the wretched huts of the peasants and serfs in the villages outside its wall. In consequence of the wealth and control accumulated by the land barons, a struggle soon developed between the king and the nobles because each noble wanted to build his own castle and conduct himself as a completely automous and independent ruler.

THE STRONG HAND OF HENRY I AND HENRY II

Amid the fervent disapproval and opposition of church officials

Henry I who ruled England from 1100-1135 worked to restrain the growing power of the land barons, he also promoted the Norman system of centralized government and gave greater authority to the royal court which initiated a feeling of English nationlism. Constant warfare between the land barons caused the general population to welcome the strong almost oppressive rule of Henry II who reigned from 1154-1189. At the height of his power Henry II ruled England and almost all of western France. His marriage to Eleanor of Aquitaine, the most famous and notorious woman of that age in western Europe brought the vast estate of the Duchy of Aquitaine under his control.

During Henry II's reign trial by jury in circuit courts was introduced to England. Henry carried on his grandfather's (Henry I) policy of limiting the power of the nobles but his humiliating downfall came when he tried to make the Roman Catholic Church in England submit to his royal authority. This policy brought him into conflict with his former friend and cohert, Thomas Beckett whom Henry himself had appointed archbishop of Canterbury. The breech between Henry and Beckett plunged the King into a deep foreboding depression whereupon four of his knights accosted Beckett while he was at vespers in the cathedral and stabbed him to death. This brought anything but relief to Henry's dilemma for each year thereafter he was required to submit to the clergy and have himself whipped while lying prostrate upon Beckett's casket. In this way was he to make amends to his former loving for according to his wife Eleanor, Henry was varied in his sexual preferences and was even known "to people his bed with sheep from time to time."[129]

In spite of his degenerate lifestyle, Henry's establishment of the common law-judicial system was a landmark in the development of the English people. Prior to this institution most disputes in western Europe were settled through trial by ordeal in which the plaintiff and defendant would meet in mortal combat and the survival of the fittest determined guilt or innocence. The courts of common law established by Henry handed down their decisions according to long standing customs, beliefs and what was held to be right or wrong by most people in the community.

THE ROOTS OF FREEMASONRY IN WESTERN EUROPE

During this period the medieval guild organizations began to development and came to be known as freemasons. This terminology was applied to guild workers because most of the laborers used to build cities and buildings were serfs (slave labor) only the skilled craftsman taught in the secret schools were called "liber" or "soc" men meaning "freeman of the craft" hence, freemasonry. Every man who dwelt in a town was not a freeman, there were no free women, but those limited few who understood the "liber" or the "craft" were the only freemen outside of the aristocracy. Also during the middle ages in Europe if a person could read and write it was considered to be proof positive that he was initiated into the priestly class, hence the term clergy.

The concept of craft and skilled workman guilds and secret societies was originally a part of the Mystery School System of Ancient Afrika as a means of perpetuating from generation to generation the practical sciences needed to sustain the High Culture Societies.

Now there is a good object lesson which can be garnered from this for Black Men and Women who are subject to the Anglo-Saxon world of today. Though we are often faced with almost insurmountable odds through the proper development or skills, crafts and sciences such as mathematics, military science, genetics, agriculture, nutrition, etc. within the framework of a correct political and cultural contest and in harmony with the spiritual (esoteric) sciences as expressed in our varies forms of religious identity i.e., Islam, Christianity, Judaism, Akan, Yuroba, and so forth, we can become the most powerful people on earth. Your natural enemy knows this quite well that is why he uses his high technology medium to keep your mind in your "behind" instead of in the center of your head where it belongs, for while you are dancing, finger popping, and gyrating your "butt" he is busy taking care of the business of the science of how to run the world. Whenever we as a people just look as though we are tired of this nonsense and are about to harken to the Divine Wisdom of the teachers sent unto us, the European controllers of mind technology drapes another fad of sensational diversion on the weak minded masses. If that doesn't work he sets about breaking up our organizations, which is sometimes relatively easy to do because of the gross ego problems existing in many of them. Unfortunately and oft times, due to many betrayals of brother against brother our natural enemy has either jailed, exiled or killed most of our legitimate leadership. Yet in the face of all this, Black People are more than able, if they will it, to arise more over destined to rise to the glorious occasion and meet the challenge of creating a new world order.

THE WHITE MAN GAINED ENTRY TO THE EAST

As you will recall shortly after Christian Rome replaced

Imperial Rome Europe passed into an era known as the dark ages or medieval times (538-1798). During this era the quest for academic knowledge was forbidden to the common people on pain of death. At this time, witchcraft and all kinds of strange, cannabalistic, blood drinking cults continued to bear sway over the ignorant masses; while the Catholic clergy kept locked up in dungeons, the original Christians, documents and teaching they had stolen from the Afrikan Church. Because of starvation, plague and over-crowded conditions the barbaric Europeans set out in the name of the so-called Christian crusades to explore, conquer and colonize north Africa and the Middle East. This subject will be discussed at length in a forthcoming work by the author entitled *A History of the Christian Church: An Afrikan World View.*

In 1906 the Roman Catholic church in western Europe inaugurated a series of five military campaigns. These expeditions, which continued intermittently until 1291, were designed to defeat the Muslims and gain entry and control of the East. In 1701 the turks invaded Byzantine territory in Asia Minor inflicting a disasterous defeat on the Christian armies. In 1081 emperor Alexius Comnenus dispatched from Constantinople (the Byzantine capital) to the leaders of European Christians in the west an urgent plea for help, imploring them to come to his aid as a fellow Christian monarch and assist in the fight against the Turks in the east. Fourteen years later in 1095 Pope Urban II, envious and coveting the opulant splendor of the great Muslim civilization which stretched from Spain in the west to China in the East, seized upon the opportunity of the Byzantine request as a means of expanding the political and economic power of the Roman Church. Anticipating the huge profits to be made from the venture he went about organizing the first of the so-called "holy crusades".

Urban travelled through the land preaching that it was the duty of western Europe to rise to occasion and come to the aid of their Christian brothers in the East, to go forth and drive out the "infidel Muslims" and liberate the tomb of Christ in Jerusalem, which was then held by the Mohammedans. Motivated by the fervent exhortations of the prelate, whom many in western Europe at that time revered as the Vicar of the very God Himself on earth, kings and knights envisioning the great wealth to be gained from the spoils of victory assembled their forces for the conquest of the "holy land". Before the end of the century tens of thousands of Europeans seeking to escape their mean existence in the west had made the long trek to the Middle East.

During the time of the Christian crusades homosexuality and pederasty (sexual abuse of young boys) was very popular and widely accepted in England. Many of the knights took their favorite little boys with them to be their sexual partners while they were away on the crusades. For these gallant "knights in shining armor", rape of women and men was matter-of-factly common. Dogs, goats, cows, pigs, geese and an astonishing variety of animals were used in the common practice of bestiality by the nobility and general populace in England and incest was epidemic.[150] This crusade despite its "holy" enthusiasm failed to break through the Mohammedan wall which stood between bleak, retarded Europe and the opulant treasurers of the Far East. Christian ships of the 11th century were unable to navigate the Red Sea nor did Europeans of the time have a sufficient enough knowledge of geography to travel overland to the Indies. Therefore the Muslims continued to control the middleman vantage point of trade to the East.

The Europeans discovered they could profit more from trading when fighting with the Muslims and the later crusades were little more than trading ventures. This change of perspective resulted in the enormous increases in wealth, prestige, and power which came to the Roman Catholic Church during the 12th, 13th, and 14th centuries. Armed with these resources the church authorities ruthlessly suppressed all opposition to their official doctrines and policies, through such institutions as the horrid and fiendish tortures of the Spanish Inquisition and the excommunication and disposition of all heretic monarchs. For a long period (until the Protestant Reformation and the French Revolution) the Popes of Rome set up and dethroned kings at their pleasure, accepted whole kingdoms as fiefs and exercised jurisdiction in the myriad international controversies which took place on the continent.

On the other hand the crusades having brough vast numbers of west Europeans into intimate contact with the superior culture of the Near and Middle East stimulated a spirit of inquiry which during the 14th and 15th centuries caused Europe to begin experiencing a period of heightened intellectual and artistic activity. Towards the end of the middle ages European artists and scholars using the methods taught to them by the Muslims began to turn from church dominated education to Greek and Roman philosophy and literature. This movement towards the rebirth of classical learning originally brought to the continent by the Moors had its inception in the wealthy seaport town of Venice. Italy and is commonly referred to by European scholars as the Renaissance.

Between 711-1258 the Moorish empire had held the sceptre of power over a great portion of the then known world. And even after its brilliant lights began to dim the influence and culture of the Muslims was still keenly felt in Europe and other places where these Blacks had ruled. Shortly after the decline of Moorish civilization in western Europe began, the Renaissance and it was during this period when Europe's backward Afrikan-trained inhabitants were seeking to find an identity that the painting, sculpture and general portrayal of biblical characters as white took place. Today as we behold these images hanging on church walls, depicted in Sunday School literature and strewn throughout family bibles, many of us do not as Rev. Cleage says, "realize that these were not statements of fact; but, statements by white men, depicting what they wanted to believe was true. I say what they wanted to believe was true, because essentially they knew that white men did not Create Christianity. They borowed it. More bluntly, they stole it."[130]

Having been titilated by the Moorish introduction of the industries and arts of Eastern lands and commodities like sugar, paper, medicinal drugs and articles of luxury, European monarchs were further enhanced by the hastened development of trade between Europe and the Middle East stimulated by the crusades. Italy's seacoast towns were the first to flourish and as a result commerce and urban life gradually spread over western Europe. The mercantile businessmen who garnered the profits from this accelerated commerical growth eventually freed themselves of the countless statutes of feudal restrictions placed upon their business transactions and began to pour large sums of money into advancing the art of shipbuilding and the study of the science of navigation. Thus was laid the basis for later European exploration and colonial expansion. This new and wealthy class of mercantile traders became potent allies of the monarchs who were constantly engaged in a struggle to subdue the aristocratic powers of the land holding feudal lords.

In closing out this chapter we would like to submit a quote by one Joseph McCabe a Caucasian historian who describes the contrast between the blight of Europe and the elegant beauty of the Moorish empire during the period we have just been discussing "None of our modern sophistry redeems the squalor of Europe from the fifth to the eleventh century. and it was again the dark-skinned men of the south who restored civilization. By the year 1000, Europe was reduced to a condition which, if we were not Europeans, we would frankly call barbarism, yet at that time, the Arabs had a splendid civilization in Spain, Sicily, Syria, Egypt and Persia, and it linked to those of India and China. We write manuals of the history of Europe, or of the Middle Ages, and we confine ourselves to a small squalid area. . . and ignore the brilliant civilization that ran from Portugal to the China Sea."[131]

Chapter Seven

England Makes An Attempt
At Becoming Civilized

CHAPTER SEVEN

ENGLAND MAKES AN ATTEMPT AT BECOMING CIVILIZED

PRELUDE

In keeping with our main purpose of information sharing and in the interest of continuity we shall proceed on our historical journey as we observe in the next few chapters the evolution of the British empire. From this point we shall steadily move forward towards the period of America's colonization on the United States revolutionary war, and the celebration of the fourth of you-lie.

RICHARD THE LION HEARTED

Richard I dubbed the loin hearted because he was as careless with his own life and safety as he was for the rights and safety of others, succeeded without challenge to the throne of his father Henry II in 1189. Despite his passionate ardor for war and danger the lion hearted Richard was also known to be quite a pussycat when it came to his lover the young King Phillip II of France. Richard, the favorite son of his adventurous and impulsive mother—Eleanor of Aquitaine, was throughout most of his life controlled and governed by her. In short he was a "mamma's boy" this may have been one of the reasons he had such a pronounced indulgence in homosexual activity, which really wasn't all that unusual during any period of European culture.

In the course of his ten year reign Richard taxed England to the utmost and squandered revenue in luxury, feasting and display. Yet the recklessness of his bravado in battle and his intense love for combat made him a hero in the eyes of the twelfth century England. Finally, as the result of a quarrel with one of his noblemen over a mess of gold, Richard was mortally wounded by an arrow and died in 1199 at the age of 43. Thus ended his vehement and sporadic reign on the throne of England.

THE MAGNA CARTA

Richard was succeeded by his younger brother John who ruled from 1199-1216. Often referred to as one of England's worst kings his reign was fraught with much opposition and distrust on the part of the nobles. During a rebellion of the land barons against King John, his 80 year old mother, Eleanor of Aquitaine, lead a force in defense of her unruly son but she was crushed and John had to come to her rescue. In 1213 the cowardly John surrendered his crown and the whole of the English kingdom in vassalage; that is servantude, to Innocent III the Pope of Rome. At this the artistocracy declared that John had overstepped the bounds of his power. The feudal lords then collected and organized their fighting forces to meet John 36 miles southeast of London at Rumnymede Meadow. John with his few supporters was overwhelmed at the site of the encampment of the barons armies and on June 15, 1215, by force of arms, King John was coerced into signing one of the most famous documents in English history, The Magna Carta (Latin for great charter).

Magna Carta with its 63 articles, originally written in Latin, is referred to by many European historians and public school textbooks as the "cornerstone of English liberty". This event marked the crude beginnings of the European brand of democracy in England, yet it did not grant liberty to all the people because the barons designed it to protect their rights and to aid them in gaining more privileges for the artistocracy. Magna Carta included the following in its lists of demands:

* the right to fair taxation—the king agreed that he could collect his taxes only by legal consent of the nobles instead of by military force.

* the right to trial by a jury of one's peers.

* the right to habeas corpus—the king promised not to hold a man in custody for any extended length of time without granting a hearing.

All these rights of course applied to the noblemen, clergy and freeman, not the majority population in England who were serfs.

Later King John repented signing the decree and appealed to the Pope of Rome who declared the charter void and excommunicated (condemned to eternal damnation) the land barons and all the citizens of London. The primate of the Roman Catholic Church then ordained his bishops in England to raise an army of French mercenaries which they did. With the aid of this army John and the majority of the religious leaders in England ravished the English nobility with fire, sword, plunder, murder and rape. In the midst of his merciless victory King John in the year 1216 was overcome with dysentery (a bowel disease) and died at the age of 49. His six year old son Henry III was crowned king by the English bishops and sat on the English throne for fifty-six years from 1216 to 1272. Because John gained such a bad reputation as a cruel, treacherous and cowardly monarch no succeeding English kings have taken his name.

Magna Carta, reputed by European textbook historians *c* *ɔe* the foundation of the democratic systems of the English spe*ɔ*k ng world could more accurately be named "the baron's law" for *ɪs* we have already observed, it defined the rights of the nobility and the ecclesiastical heads more so than that of the common people. Th is is the attitude which later characterized the land holding "gentlem n of Virginia" and the merchants of New England who formed the nu᷍ leus of the patriots of the American Revolution. This exclusivity o᷍ ' the upper class which was a carry over from the "privileged cla*ɛ* *ɜ*" of European aristocracy is one of the reasons for the lack of patri᷍ ᷍tism and participation on the part of the common white folks of the th᷍ ᷍rteen colonies during America's struggle with England. Having n᷍ land holding or business interest they considerered themselves t᷍ have nothing to gain or lose from its outcome, a fact which we shall ex᷍ ᷍mine more closely in the succeeding chapters. The Black slave and th᷍ white indentured servant made up the American serfdom and the slave smugglers along with the plantation owning slave holders, the new transplanted "privileged class."

AFRIKAN CONSTITUTIONAL SYSTEM VS. MAGNA CARTA

Magna Carta was essentially a English constitutional oligarchy (the few ruling the many) as opposed to the more enlightened constitutional system of Afrikan empires largely ruled by true democratic republics. For instance during this and most periods in English history the land legally belonged to the king and was held for him in strict vassalage by the noblemen. The Magna Carta was a step in the direction of reversing this order, yet and still feudal law bore down heavily, often brutally, on England's majority serf population. Crimes (including murder) of the free man against a serf were usually punishable by a fine. Crimes (even petty ones) of the serf against a freeman or the nobility were severely punishable usually be death. In stark contrast to this most of the nations on the mother continent were governed by the Afrikan Constitutional System, this was the law of the land and was for the protection of all the people. The Afrikan Constitutional System in use every since the dawn of recorded history held that each man was his brother's keeper and that noon should languish in need while others had. It also stated that all of the people in the society great or small were equally protected by its aegis. Here are a few of the precepts of this age old system of Afrikan juris prudence:

* the will of the people is the supreme law

* the land belongs to no individual, it is the gift of God to the collective and the king acting as steward must supervise its protection.

* all monies, gifts, taxes and resources under the stewardship of the chief or king belongs to the collective and is to be used to meet the needs of the people.

* the unequivocal right to equal protection of the law for all classes of the society.

For a detailed study of the Afrikan Constitutional System and its wonderful effects on the quality of life of the people ead *The Destruction of Black Civilization*, Chapter VI by Dr. Chancellor Williams.[132]

THE BEGINNINGS OF THE ENGLISH PARLIAMENT

Henry III, the eldest son of King John and a grandson of Henry II, came to the throne of England in 1216 when he was only nine years old, but he did not actually rule until he was twenty in 1227. Henry III is described as a fickle tyrant who surrounded himself with favorites from other countries. The foreign influences in Henry's court incited the English nobility to revolt against his rule and enforced the provisions of the Magna Carta to limit his revenue.

In desperation to raise more capital than the land barons would vote him, Henry in 1254 summoned the great council which came to be known as the Provisions of Oxford. This custom of English kings, summoning assemblies of leading churchmen and the aristocracy to discuss government problems, especially in times of grave crisis, dated back to the Witan (Council of the Wise Men) of Aglo-Saxon times, Monarch's chiefly employed these assemblies for the purpose of augumenting the revenues and adding to the products of their domain by way of the taxes which the assembly consented to levy on their subjects. At this meeting Henry III, because of his weak economic status, was forced to transfer governing powers to a committee of barons and churchmen whom he agreed would have the legal right to override his decisions.

Later, in 1261, when Henry broke the agreement of the Provisions of Oxford the barons rose up in revolt and made war on the king. The leader of this revolt, one Simon de Monfort defeated Henry III in the battle of Lewes and imprisoned him in the year 1264. To govern the country de Monfort in 1265 summoned a council that included not only barons and churchmen, but also knights and representative of counties and towns. This assembly called de Monfort's Parliament was a major step in the development of the English parliamentary system. Simon, the leader of the reformed party, then governed England until he was killed at the battle of Evesham in 1265 by Henry's son, Edward I, who after his crushing victory at the battle of Evesham continued to dominate the government during the rest of his father's feeble lifetime. In 1270 Edward joined the last crusade in Palestine but finally had to give up the losing fight against the Muslims. While away, due to the death of his father, Henry III, he became King in 1272.

After returning to England in 1274 Edward I carried out many legal reforms he compelled the church courts to confine their judgments to religious cases only and forbade further grants of land to the church without royal consent. In 1290 he ordered all Jews, some 16,000, to leave England. Edward confirmed the Magna Carta and agreed not to collect taxes without the consent of Parliament. During his reign trade grew and towns prospered, the king strengthened the royal court and England started its long upward climb towards becoming a center of learning in Europe. Of this period in English history Durant writes:

> "Cleanliness in the Middle Ages was not next go godliness. Early Christianity had denounced the Roman baths as wells of perversion and promiscuity, and its general disapproval of the body had put no premium on hygiene...One result of the crusades was the introduction into Europe of public steambaths in the Moslem style. The Church frowned upon public baths as leading to immorality'...Monasteries, feudal castles, and rich homes had latrines, emptying into cesspools, but most homes managed with outhouses; and in many cases one outhouse had to serve a dozen homes. Pipes for carrying waste were one of the sanitary reforms introduced into England by Edward I...In the thirteenth century the chamber pots of Paris were freely emptied from windows into the streets, with only a warning cry."[132]

Also at the time of Edward I's reign carpets and tapestries were brought to England from Moorish Spain in 1254 by his wife Eleanor of Castile and became fashionable in the rancid home of the aristocracy.

In order to raise money for his constant wars with Scotland, Edward called an assembly in 1295. This Parliament consisted of representatives from the nobility, the church, and the common people as well. This system of representation, which embraced the entire country, set a model for later Parliamentarian and is known in English history as the Model Parliament, the word "Parliament"a from a French term meaning "speaking conference". The Model Parliament is considered by white historians to be the fore runner of what they call "the most democratic representative government in the world" but as we have seen this simply is not so. The Afrikan Constitutional System is the oldest and most democratic system of government known to man. At this Model Parliament, Edward restricted the power of the king by accepting the rule that taxes could be levied and laws made only with the consent of a majority vote in Parliament. He also sponsored laws aimed at destroying the feudal system of the land barons and limiting the awesome ecclesiastical power of the Roman Church.

Having failed at his life's ambition, which was to conquer Scotland, Edward I died July 7, 1307 at the age of 70 and was succeeded by his weak son, Edward II. At the death of Edward I, which was 241 years after the Norman conquest, the whole population of England and Wales was estimated at three million, three-quarters of the people were peasants and most of these were serfs. At this time most of Europe was berft of advanced agricultural and industrial techniques such as those applied by the Moors in the south throughout this study. We keep presenting this contrast because we want you to get a true picture of the real Europe whose descendents dominate and control nearly every phase of the black Man's life today.

The striking examples of white peoples moral backwardness and "numerical inadequacies" spoken of by Dr. Frances Welsing in her revelatory study entitled *The Cress Theory of Color Confrontation* was aided in part by the constant assault of famine disease and war which with exacting and uninterrupted continuity plagued caucasian Europe throughout its history.[134] In 14th century England a bitter poverty abounded beggers and thieves were so numerous and commonplace as to organize themselves into guilds to protect and govern their profession. The majority of the population suffered from gout, asthma, rheumatism, siatica, tuberculosis, dropsy and gross diseases of the eyes and skin. Very few members of the populous reached the age of forty and still fewer that of fifty. It was against this background that such institutions as the Parliament (the English Senate) was established and nurtured to a point where it eventually became the model for the United States Senate and its constitutional system. Considering the overwhelming circumstances and innate characteristics of the caucasian and his Euro-American descendants, I must in all fairness say that this was an almost miraculous achievement for him and his progeny, and although, even unto this day, they have never learned how to put into practice the high ideals of such institutions it was nevertheless a nice sentiment and a good attempt at being civilized.

As Europeans emerged from their shadowy world they took their agitated, contentious and disease ridden way of life with them to other lands. Most of these lands were inhabited by the 87% population of people of color on the Planet Earth, who by comparison to the gross estate of European society at that time were the torchbearers of enlightenment and humane principles in the world. Very few of these sun people were fully cognizant of or even prepared for the European's religious devotion to war, pestilance and strife. Consequently we behold the state of the Planet Earth such as it is today. No my beloved Black brothers and sisters, this statement is not a manifestation of "racism in reverse" but the undeniable edict of the white man's record of his own history. For the facts that I am presenting here can be found in many encyclopedias and scholarly works of European history, especially those which strive for "realism". [135] The degenerate condition of Europe's diseased inhabitants persisted steadily from century to century and was still prominent during the period of their exploration and colonial expansion, in fact by the time of the revolutionary war of 1776 it seems like that most of Europe's mass population would remain in this state forever. Had it not been for the huge fortunes of the AFrikan slave trade and their colonial holdings. Europe probably would be in that same condition today.

English Parliamentary law which later became the foundation for the United States legislative system was based on the Roman senate system of preserving the rights of all Roman citizens, which they inherited from the republican ideal of the Greek City states generally accredited to Plato and Socrates. Yet the most permanent institutions of humanisn and the rights of the common man are rooted and grounded in the exalted morals of the High Culture Civilizations of the Ancient Afrikans.

THE ENGLISH INQUISITION

Edward II who reigned from 1307-1327 unlike his father was weak and incompetent, always steered by the will of others. It is said that he was destitute of any seriousness of thought and cared for nothing but amusing himself. Seeking to redeem his shallow image and lack of prestige in the eyes of the English people, Edward II set about on a half-hearted attempt to fulfill his father's life long dream of conquering Scotland. In the year 1314 Edward at the head of a large army invaded Scotland but as a result of his incompetence and lack of preparedness his force was thoroughly beaten by the military cunning of Robert Bruce at the Battle of Bannockburn. The baron's viewed Edward's failure to take Scotland as the "last straw" and once more turned against the king. Unmoved by all this the sovereign returned to a carefree life of fun and games and left the governing of the kingdom to his greedy playmate cronies.

On June 20, 1327 Parliament edged on by Edward's wife, Queen Isabelle and her lover Roger Mortimer forced Edward to abdicate (to give up) the throne in favor of his young son, Edward III. While trying to escape England by way of the North Sea, Edward II was arrested and imprisoned at Kenilworth Castle where he was systematically ill-treated with every imaginable indignity inflicted upon him in hopes that he would die of disease. After withtstanding the ill treatment of his enemies for over eight months, on September 21, 1327 he was cruelly put to death at the orders of the queen and her paramour.

Most historians agree that torture was not normally employed as a means of interrogation in England. But in the case of the weak and vacillating Edward II the method was applied to force confessions of treason and heresy (beliefs contrary to the doctrines of the Roman Church) from a group of Templars (freemasons). At first Edward was hesitant to use inquisitional torture but when Clement V, the Pope of Rome wrote him a letter stating "We hear that you forbid torture as contrary to the laws of your land. But no state can override cannon law, our law. Therefore I command you at once to submit these men to torture."[136] Unpon receipt of this letter Edward II hastened to carry out the orders of his Roman master. Such was the power of the bishops of the Roman Catholic Church over the sovereign states of Europe in those days.

At this point let us stop here for a word concerning the Knights of the Templars once of the parent orders from which developed Europe's so-called freemasons. Many of the ideas and rituals used in the Masonic order stemmed from the period of cathedral building which took place between the 900's and 1600's. The fraternal guilds of Europe's skilled craftsmen later developed into the lodges of the 1700's. In principle the Masonic lodges are merely bastardized attempts at reviving in Europe the remnants of the High Science of the Afrikan Mystery Schools which had been closed by Justinian I in the 6th century C.E. This resurgence of European interest in the most ancient sciences was rekindled during the period of the crusades in which the Knights of the Templars was one of the main participants. The 32nd and 33rd degree Masons of the Ancient, Arabic Order of

Nobles of the Mystic Shrine are in substance the white man's attempt at being a closet Muslim. The original Afrikan High Science which required forty-seven years to attain the 360 degrees to which the European Masons are seeking to iniate themselves, is as it were a billion galaxies out of their reach for as the Last Poets remind us "33 degrees is as far as the white man can go without falling apart".[137]

The Masons of today (organized 1777) are a formation of the Grand Lodge of England which is the Mecca of this fraternal society. For more details on the original Afrikan High Culture Science as the foundation of modern European Masonry and its symbolism see *Afrika, Mother of Western Civilization* by Dr. Yosef ben Jochannon, pages 436-452 and the entire text of *They All Look Alike* by the same author.[138]

THE GLORIES OF MOORISH CIVILIZATION

In 1300 England was ninety percent rural, the largest town was London with a population of 40,000 and living conditions were pretty much the same as they were in 1000. Although recorded sanitation laws were a little stricter the people persisted in dumping their garbage and slops from the window unto the streets. A general condition of dirt and squalor continued to permeate Europe even unto Russia. This is why there were so many epidemics and plagues which so often ran rampant throughout European history.

During this same period, a fact which some white writers try to "hopscotch" around, between 1248 and 1354 in the kingdom of Granada the Moors were building the Alhambra described by witnesses of the time as a wonderland of palaces, unequaled in the history of architecture. It was the finest example of architectural beauty in all of Europe. Here at the Alhambra Afrikans conducted classes in high science and learning amid the perfumed gardens made musical with the sounds of many fabulous fountains and the songs of nightingales floating upon Mediterranean evening breezes. Also at this same time the Moorish city of Cordoba, almost a half millenium (500 years old) was still thriving. Among its many wonders was a great mosque with more than 1,000 pillars of granite, onyx, marble, jasper and other precious stones supporting its arches. Then there was the city of Seville with its network of shaded streets, white-washed balconied houses built around luxuriant courtyards and fine park areas with beautiful fountains spread throuhgout the city for the enjoyment of all classes. This is just a cameo picture of the magnificent Moorish civilization which ruled and influenced southwestern Europe in those days. All this and more "was hundreds of years old before there was a paved street in Paris or even a street lamp in London." [139]

Chapter Eight

"Wars And Rumors of Wars"

CHAPTER EIGHT

"WARS AND RUMORS OF WARS"

THE HUNDRED YEARS WAR

The Hundred Years War was a series of armed conflicts which took place 1337-1453 between England and France, the battles were fought on French soil. Edward III of England whose mother was a sister of Charles IV the late king of France began the war by disputing the Right of Phillip VI, cousin of the deceased Charles, to sit on the throne of France.

Edward insisted upon claiming sovereignty over France but the French were resolved that no English king would rule them and the struggle ensued. Edward III was the official rule of England from 1327-1377, he was placed on the throne at the age of fourteen after his father, Edward II was forced to abdicate. For nearly three years his mother Isabelle and her lover Robert Mortimer were the real rules of England. In 1330 at the age of seventeen the young king arrested his mother and had Mortimer put to death on the charge of murdering his father, then he began to rule England in his own right.

In preparation for the war with France Edward and his armies crossed the English channel and landed in Normandy. In 1346 the first major engagement of the Hundred Years War was fought at the battle of Crecy, a little Frendh village off the coast of the English Channel. On August 26 the English scored a great victory, but Phillip VI king of France stood his ground until only six of his soldiers were left on the field. Approximately 30,000 men were killed in this one engagement. For the first time in the history of European warfare cannons, which had been developed by a German priest in 1313, were used on a small scale in this battle, thus dooming the military effectiveness of the feudal knight and his castle and opening a new and more destructive phase of warfare. The method of casting forth projectiles by means of gunpowder blast, as used in the primitive artillery at the battle of Crecy, was unknown by Europeans until it was brought back from the east by Marco Polo. In China this substance was primarily used in fireworks to entertain people, not to kill them. Surely everything the caucasian touches becomes an instrument of death. In this battle French knights clad in armor on horseback were defeated by English foot soldiers, this ended the supremacy of mounted knights in battle and sounded the death knoll of feudalism as an effective system in European warfare, thereafter England, France and Western European nations began to organize and maintain professional standing armies. The victory at Crecy established England as a formidable military power for the first time.

In 1360 Edward III gave up his claim to the French throne and signed a peace treaty at Bretigny, France. In 1369 was again broke out between England and France but this time the English armies met with ruinous defeat, England lost most of its French possessions and the economy was exhausted. By 1375 Edward II was forced to withdraw from the struggle. Edward's reign ended in failure to make good his claim tothe French throne and maintain England's territorial holdings in France. At his death in 1377 his grandson Richard II came to the throne. Because Edward III had been more interested in war during his reign than in internal government, Parliament—that ominous body of lawmakers who during England's later colonial expansion, would vote the passing of many bills condemning untold millions of Afrikans to slavery and death gained new powers and became established as a permanent part of the English government.

THE PLAGUE OF BLACK DEATH

Between 1347 and 1550 the bubonic plague called the black death because of the dark spots it left on the skin of its victims killed approximately one-third Europe's population. The bubonic plague came primarily from rats, secondary from man and largely as a result of all the wars in Europe which caused starvation, disease and devastation. When the black death struck Europe was completely helpless to combat it, there was no natural immunity to the disease and the standard of public health and personal hygeine was nearly nonexistent. Except in those areas that were controlled by the advanced medical science of the Moorish empire. The backward medical profession in western Europe at the time was no match for the pestilence and its usual treatments of syphoning blood and attaching leeches to the body were made even more absurd in the face of this terrible calamity.

In 1338 the black death struck England and killed about one-third to one-half of its population. According to Durant "the epidemic had effects in every sphere in life...the immensity of the suffering and the tragedy weakened many minds, producing contagious neurosis; whole groups seemed to go mad in unison, like the Flagellants who in 1349,...marched through the city streets almost naked, beating themselves in penitence, preaching the Last Judgement..."[140]

THE WAT TYLER REBELLION

After the Hundred Years War had been going on for forty-four years there arose in the days of Richard II a peoples revolt called Wat Tyler's Rebellion. This uprising of English farm laborers occurred in the year 1381 when King Richard II was only 14 years of age. It was a result of the extremely heavy taxation on the peasantry, who also objected to the harsh conditions under which they lived, such as forced labor. On June 12th, Wat Tyler leading an angry mob of about 100,000 peasants marched on London and demanded to see the King. Richard's royal advisors deserted him and he was left to face the belligerent mob alone. Unable to quiet the riotous crowd he finally agreed to listen to their demands.

Overwhelmed by the circumstances the boy-king afreed to their terms which included an end to serfdom (slavery), a repeal of the oppressive labor laws, low rental payments on freed lands and a general amnesty for all those who participated in the revolt. Richard agreed, thirty clerks were at once set to work drawing up official documents validating the covenant, but the one ultimatum the fourteen year old sovereign refused to agree to was the demand that certain ministers of his cabinet should be handed over to the people, as traitors, to be disposed of according to their will. Instead Richard promised that all persons accused of misconduct in government would be tried by the orderly processes of the law of the land and would be duly punished if found guilt. Most of the rioters accepted these terms and began to disband, going their separate ways.

Wat Tyler was not pleased with the decision and in protest marched through the streets at the head of a band of about 30,000 peasants wielding pitchforks, axes, clubs and whatever else they could find. This unwielding group went to the Tower of London and there discovered one of Richard's advisors praying in the chapel, the mob dragged the aristocratic clergyman out into the courtyard where an amateur executioners ax severed his head from his body whereupon they affixed the archbishop's miter firmly upon his head by driving a nail through his skull. Finding and beheading three others they then mounted all the heads on pines and carried them in ceremonial procession, amid the shouts and jeers of the unruly crown, through the city of London and affixed the blood dripping spectacles over the gates of the London Bridge. As the gourged and lacerated heads set in silent vigil above little pools of blood the crowd spent the rest of the day in gleeful slaugher.

At a meeting of negotiations with the king and his nobles Wat Tyler was struck down by London's mayor and killed by one of Richard's squires. The king' s troops arrived and drove the remaining rebels away and on July 2,

1381 the head of Wat Tyler along with those of some of the leading of the revolt adorned the gate of the London Bridge and the stink of their decay floated upon the air for weeks. Young King Richard's promises were put aside and the oppression and heavy taxation of the peasants continued.

Richard III began his 22 year reign in 1377, his constant struggle with Parliament and poor administration of the country caused the people to turn against him. In 1399 Richard hated of all classes of the English people, because of his extravagance and outrageous conduct, was at the age of thirty-two forced to abdicate the throne and sent to prison where one year later he was undoubtedly murdered by his successor and engineer of the plot Henry IV.

During the reign of Henry IV (1399-1413) the conflict with France was renewed and this protracted warfare continued throughout the reign of Henry V (1413-1422) and unto the latter part of the reign of Henry VI (1422-1461). In 1431 the English were ignominiously defeated by the French armies under the command of Joan of Arc. Joan was finally captured by Henry V's French allies and sold to the English. She was then tried in a kangaroo court and sentenced to be burned at the stake as a witch. On May 30, 1331 thousands of people gathered at the marketplace in the city of Rouen, France and witnessed her frail body burning amid the flames of the smoking pyres. English military commanders jubiliantly gloated her demise as her ashes were gathered up and thrown into the Seine River. From this point the hundred years war dallied in reluctant truce while the decimated ranks of the infantry were replenished with men too poor to value life at more than a few dollars above death.

Through the years the English won most of the battles but the French finally won the war. By the time the war ended during the reign of Henry VI in 1453, England had lost all its territorial holdings in France with the exceptions of Calais a small city just 25 miles across the English Channel. The events of the hundred years war resulted in the development of new military tactics and the groowth of English sea power which eventually rivaled that of Spain for in those days Spain was the foremost sea power in western Europe having inherited this status from the Moorish kings.

THE WARS OF THE ROSES

The smoke and clamor of the hundred years war was still swirling in the minds of the people one year after its official termination when the Wars of the Roses broke out in 1454 lasting some 31 years this war was a struggle between the house (family) of Lancaster whose emblem was a red rose and the house of York who chose the symbol of a white rose. Here again we view the constant strife between the king and the land barons being manifested in this particular conflict. King Henry VI of the Lancaster family was a weak and feeble ruler and the nobles of the family of York rose in arms against him. The soldiers of each camp roamed about the countryside looting villages and towns and murdering without remorse all who stood in their way. Edward IV of the house of York decreed that no captives should be taken alive. The tame and gentle Henry IV was reluctant to fight the war so his vigorous Queen Margaret of Anjou vicariously led the kings forces in fierce resistance to Edward's army, but was defeated in 1461. Edward IV then became king of England (1461-1470).

Edward ignored Parliament and extorted gifts of money from his subjects, which were largely used to support his life of wine, women and song. The governing of the kingdom was left to one Richard Neville Earl of Warwick. Warwick gained such respect and honor from the people to incite Edward to jealousy. The king then viciously turned on his former favorite whereupon the estranged Warwick united with the army of the red rose party under the leadership of Queen Margaret, The collaborate forces ran Edward out of the country, and in 1470 restored Henry VI to the throne.

Aided by French land barons Edward organized an army, returned to England, killed Warwick in battle, defeated Margaret once again, had her imprisoned in the Tower of London and on May 22, 1471 ordered the murder of Henry VI. Edward then seized the throne and reigned another twelve years. In the spring of 1483 Edward IV died and his oldest son Edward V at the age of twelve became king. His uncle Richard seized the boy sovereign and his nine year old brother, had them locked up in the Tower of London and on July 6, 1483 the hunched back, ill featured Richard II limped up to the throne and had himself crowned king. Nine days later Edward V and his younger brother were clandestinely smothered to death with pillows leaving Richard III to rule, so he thought, without protest.

In 1485 after less than two years on the throne, Richard III on a dark foreboding day in August met the forces of Henry Tudor, of the House of Lancaster, at the battle of Bosworth Field. Destitute of popular support and deserted by his soldiers Richard greatly outnumbered was knocked from his horse, arising in a fit of desperate rage he challenged Tudor's army in a one-man charge and was mortally wounded. Later that afternoon Richard III's deformed body dangling face down across the back of his horse was paraded through the land amid shouting curses of derision and shame. Henry Tudor of the red rose party (house of Lancaster) was then crowned Henry VII king of England and married Countess Elizabeth of the House of York (white rose party) thus ended the Wars of the Roses which left England's diseased and starving masses even more desolate and impoverished than when it began.

Hnery VII's absolute rule (1485-1509) subordinated the clergy, subdued the barons and firmly disciplined the merchants. When he came to the throne England's resources were sorely depleted and the country was in a perpetual state of feudal unrest and anarchy. During his reign however England first turned its eyes towards America and colonial expansion. For more details see *Afrikan People and European Holidays: A Mental Genocide*, Book I, pages 32-33. As a result of Henry's hearty support of the mercantile colonial traders interest and his tight-fisted handling of money, upon his death the sly, shrewd, tough, cold-blooded and paramoid Henry VII left to his son Henry VIII a strong, stable and solvent kingdom.

During the Tudor age intiated by the reign of Henry VII the speech of the populace was course and profane. Violence was the standard way of life and each citizen was his own policeman ever ready to fight and kill, with a steady stomach, at the slightest provocation. More than 130 years of constant warfare had further escalated the inate brutal and reckless dog-eat-dog nature of the English people. Theft was as commonplace as breathing itself and commercial frauds almost ruined England's foreign trade. Because of poor farming techniques vegetables were scarce in fact they were undesirable and flesh of all kinds was the national food. Not given to drinking water, each person including the clergy drank at least a gallon of beer a day for beer and ale were the national drinks of England.

Women wore head covering and men even among the aristocracy wore their hats at the dinner table to keep their long, dirty and unkept hair from getting into the food. Having as yet no knowledge of the handkerchief men and women wiped their noses on their sleeves or blew them by hand onto the floor or street. There being no such things as napkins on the table the dinners often wiped their greasy hands and cleaned their teeth on the ends of tablecloths. All food was eaten by hand. The men of the aristocracy sometimes hid their unkept unwashed hair under powdered wigs and draned tight silk stockings and skin tight pants to display their flat buttocks, which as one English ecclesiastic writer of the period has said made them look like "the hinder part of a she-ape in the full of moon".

In regards to the king's castle despite its cosmetic elegant decor and ornamental surroundings Durant quotes an observer of the times as stating "Almost all the floors are of clay and rushes from the marshes, so carelessly renewed that the foundation sometimes remains for twenty years, harboring, there below, spittle and vomit and wine (urine) of dogs and men, beer...remnants of fishes, and other filth unnamable. Hence, with the change of weather a vapor exhaled which in my judgment is far from wholesome."[141] This was 15th and 16th century England as it slowly and steadily began to spread its morals and manners around the earth through exploration and colonial expansion.

FOUNDATION OF THE AFRIKAN SLAVE TRADE

In 1492 the Moors undermined by the so-called Jews were expelled from their last stronghold in Granada. The Moors had arrived eight centuries earlier in Spain and brought with them the science and ethics of the Ancient Afrikan High Culture System which included the principles of liberty, justice and religious freedom for all. From these ideals were later to develop in Europe and French and German philosophies of humanism which were supposed to be the foundations of the Protestant Reformation and other so-called forms of European enlightenment. What these new schools of thought were in essence was an attempt at reviving the high moral ethics of the Egyptian Mystery System in the context of Europe's political needs.

During the 1400's and 1500's Spain and Portugal due to the benefits of the opulant and learned presence of the former Moorish domination there, were among the first nations to establish strong central governments, they ranked as the most powerful nations in Europe. At that time Spain and Portugal dominated the sea and the field of explotation. Under the direction of Prince Henry the navigator and King John II Portugal set itself the task of finding new trade routes to the Indies by means of the unknown Atlantic Ocean. Portugese ships travelled down the west coast of Afrika, establishing a number of coastal trading posts. In 1441 they captured four of the Mother Continents beautiful Black sons and took them back to Portugal, then began the saga of Europe's depopulation and eventual control of the heartland of Planet Earth, the continent of Afrika. It from this point on that the world began to understand, as is so fitting set forth in the immortal lyrics of Minister Louis Farrakhan's composition *The White Man's Heaven is the Black Man's Hell.*

Meanwhile in the Afrikan interior the tall Black and strong willed Sunni Ali the Great (1464-1492) was laying the foundation for the mighty Songhai Empire, a subject we will be discussing with more detail in a forth coming work entitled *Afrika the Source of All Enlightenment.*

In the past chapters we have stayed somewhat close to the chronological details of the primary events which contributed to the evolution of England as a world power. This information was presented in this manner so that the reader could get a close up view of the people who were number one in bringing about the demise of the Afrikan and as a means of documenting the gross lifestyles and mentality of those degenerate people whose nation eventually became the leading slave merchants in the western world. In the next chapters we will be primarily concerned with presenting personalities and events from the viewpoint of how England grew to such a vantage position as to enable them to colonize so much of the Black and colored world.

Chapter Nine

The Protestant Reformation and The Afrikan Slave Trade

CHAPTER NINE

THE PROTESTANT REFORMATION AND THE AFRIKAN SLAVE TRADE

THE ENGLISH REFORMATION

In Book I. *Afrikan People and European Holidays: A Mental Genocide*, Chapter I we have already examined the real underlying principles of the Protestant Reformation in Europe in general and England in particular. Following is a few additional observations on the subject.

The violent upheavals of the Protestant Reformation stem in part from the intellectual movement of the Renaissance period in Europe which eventually fermented into total rebellion against the Roman Catholic ecclesiastical powers and the church's total hold on what little was left of the people's minds. In the Papal controlled Europe of the 16th century Protestantism was an energetic new idea which seemed to promise relief to the deranged and suffering peasant masses. At first it started out as a reform movement to restore discipline in the Roman Church but later erupted into a full-fledged revolt and rejection of Papal authority.

It was a time when men were burned at the stake for questioning or denying the divinity of Christ. A time when manufacturers with the blessings and approval of the Roman Catholic Church cruelly exploited the cheap labor of the masses. An era when the mercantile interests of the new landlords quadrupled the cost of renting shabby, rundown, filth-ridden tenements. Because of low wages and high prices most of the peasantry unable to pay the extorted fees lost their leases and thousands upon thousands of those rendered homeless made their way to London and other cities to become beggers or to eke out the rest of their existence in petty thievery and a life of crime. All this took place amid the fervent preachings of the Roman Church representing itself as God's kingdom on earth that the peasantry should humbly and cheerfully accept the benign disposition of God's will for there to be an aristocracy and the divine right of kings.

Again I am compelled to stop here and remind you these are the pale creatures who came to West Afrika enslaved our immediate ancestors and all but destroyed the high moral fabric of the societies which has existed there from time immortal. This is what you celebrate when you observe European holidays.

Enter Henry VIII, the most famous personage of the English Reformation. Initially Henry was opposed to Martin Luther and the German arm of the Reformation and stated his disapproval thusly

"What serpent so venomous as he who calls the Pope's authority tyrannous?... what a great limb of the devil he is, endeavoring to tear the christian members of Christ from their head no punishment could be too great for one who will obey the chief priest and supreme judge on earth for the whole church is subject not only to Christ but...to Christ's only vicar the Pope of Rome." Luther's reply was as follows: "That lubberly ass, that frantic madman...that King of Lies, King Heintz (Henry), by God's disgrace King of England...Since with malice aforethought that damnable and rotten worm has lied against my King in heaven it is right for me to bespatter this English monarch with his own filth."[142] Such was the Christian brotherly love manifested between the two opposing denominations of "the body of Christ" in Europe. A few years later Henry himself locked horns with "God's vicar on earth" when Pope Clement VII refused to grant him a divorce from Catherine of Aragon. In beligerent rebellion Henry separated England from its Roman master, commandeered all the churchs wealth and property, established the Anglican church with Henry VIII as its head and protector and thus made himself the most absolute monarch that England had ever known. For more details on this subject read Chapter I, Book I *Afrikan People and European Holidays: A Mental Genocie.*

Those who opposed or doubted Henry's protestant move were beheaded. One of the most celebrated of the victims who tasted the King's wrath was Sir Thomas Moore. Rogers says of the name Moore "...that the best proof of the Negro origin of some of these noble British families are "the thick-lipped Moors" on their coat-of-arms. Some of these families are still named Moore."[143] In *Nature Knows No Color Line* (a title I sorely disagree with) pages 95-107 Rogers shows an impressive array of these coats-of-arms.[144]

In 1534 the English Parliament declared that the Pope of Rome had no authority in England and made the Anglican church a separate and distinct institution with King Henry the VIII as its supreme head. But even afer his split with the Roman Church, Henry still considered himself a devout catholic. From the confiscated wealth of ecclesiastical holdings Henry VIII built the first permanent Royal Navy, which cleared the coast and English channels of pirates and prepared the way for the naval victories of his daughter Elizabeth. Henry's flagship at that time was named the Mary Rose, he was terribly proud of her and planned to conquer France with his naval fleet. On setting sail for France the Mary Rose was sunk and Henry watched her slowly descend into the English Channel with approximately 600 persons aboard. Down to the depth of this watering grave also went Henry's dream of conquering France. It is said that this aquatic calamity was caused by Ann Boleyn whom the superstitutious English believed to be a witch with three breasts. They believed she had bewitched Henry into marrying her and upon being imprisoned and condemned to execution she placed a curse on Henry's ship, the Mary Rose. Actually she wanted to put the curse on the royal line of Henry VIII's descendants but since her daughter Elizabeth was in that line she decided to curse the Mary Rose and Henry's dream of conquering France. Recently Prince Charles of England has raised the hull of King Henry's Mary Rose.

Prior to the Protestant Reformation the Roman Catholic Church had always been successful at crushing rebellions against it by way of the hideous tortures of the inquisition, but the survival of the Reformation was largely due to the support of those monarchs who were in a constant struggle with the Pope of Rome. Before the reign of Henry VII and VIII in England the Roan churches ecclesiastical law held sway over all secular legislation. Henry VIII's rebellion against his spiritual father completely reversed this policy. The Protestant Reformation did incalcucable damage to the Roman Catholic Church, depriving it of many of its strong holds in western Europe and seriously impairing the churches position in other regions. The Reformation encourged bold and ruthless men to win a continent and spread the base of their Moorish inheritence of education and self-government until it reached across the Atlantic and blossomed into the high-sounding "ideals" of America's Declaration of Independence.

ELIZABETH I AND THE SPANISH ARMADA

We have previously discussed the impact of the Elizabethan age on the destiny of Afrikan People, in Book I, pages 4-6, 34-36 of this same series. Here we shall further investigate why the comman of the sea was so important to England's economic growth and colonial expansion. But first let us examine more closely the profile of the woman who engineered the demise of Spain's power at sea and swelled her coffers with blood money from the Afrikan slave trade. The caustic and flirtatious "virgin queen" Elizabeth never married because of her inability to conceive and bear seed. This was due to her genetic inherit-ence of Henry VIII's syphyllis. [145] Among other maladies she suffered from gout (painful inflammation of the joints) and had a mouth full of black teeth the result of her endless indulgence in the eating of sweets.

One of Elizabeths main favorites was the bisexual (mostly preferring men to women) William Shakespeare whom she delighted in inviting to her social functions because of his "faggot" wit for he was known to undauntedly reveal the skeletons in the closets of the lords and ladies at court. [147] In an attempt to hide her uncleanliness and lack of physical attractiveness the usually stingy Elizabeth spent extravagant sums on dresses, cosmetics and finery which she had imported from the Orient. Those who moved about in her inner-circle at court were wont to step back as she began to speak because very often in her lisping, spit would spray on all those in her immediate presence. On one occasion she spat on an expensive coat belonging to one of her cabinet members and ruined it. [146]

Elizabeth distrusted Roman Catholicism as a foreign power that might lead Englishmen to put loyalty to the church above allegiance to the queen. Therefore she firmly established the Protestant policies of her father. This strong political move caused Pope Pius V to excommunicate Elizabeth I from the "blessed community" of the "holy church" and one of his cardinals dubbed her a depraved, accursed, incesteous bastard . . . a chief of sin and abomnation in this age."

THE WAR OF THE SPANISH ARMADA

Spain had risen to power by grace of the wealth confiscated from the Moors, the voyages of Columbus and the decrees of Pope Alexander VI in 1493 which awarded Spain nearly all of the Americas for the purposes of exploitation and colonization. In consequence of these decrees and subsequent voyages of European explorers the Mediterranean ceased to be the center of the white man's commerical activity and the age of colonization was set into motion. In the 1580's while French exploration was stunted by civil war Spain had hundreds of colonies in America and England had none. Every year vast amounts of riches passed from the slave labored mines of South America to Spain and it seemed highly improbable that Spain could ever be displaced from her position of imminence in the New World.

An ongoing quarrel between Protestant England and Catholic Spain had been steadily growing since the early days of Elizabeth's reign and culminated in the death of Mary, Queen of Scots (a catholic monarch in league with Spain) whom the English government beheaded February 8, 1587. In retaliation to this act and intent on restoring Roman Catholicism in England, Phillip II of Spain with blessings and a pledge at seven and one-half million dollars from Pope Sixtus V ordered his best admiral to build and gather the largest armada (fleet of ships) ever known in European history and prepared for the invastion of England. Upon hearing of this one of Elizabeth's "seadogs" Sir Francis Drake urged the stingy sovereign to give him a fleet to head off the armada before it grew strong enough to invade England. He reminded her that now the time had come to spend some of the money she had massed through skimping, hoarding and cheating over the past thirty years. Elizabeth finally agreed to let him have thirty ships and on April 7, 1587 he quickly sailed from the port of Plymouth before the queen could change her mind, which she did but it was too late, Drake was gone. The merchants who were benefiting so handsomely from the commerce at sea donated thirty ships. Privateers (private owners of sea craft) also contributed their personal service and vessels to the fleet of the Royal Navy, by July the English had organized a fleet of 82 ships.

Meanwhile on the morning of May 29, 1588 a fleet or more that 130 war vessels set sail from Lisbon, Spain accompanied by hundreds of catholic monks under the command of the Vicar General of the Inquisition (the torture squad). The Spanish Armada arrived in the English channel July 19, 1588 and two days later the battle was on. The maneuverability of the English vessels and the superior accuracy of their firepower broke the lines of the Spanish Armada, the English set fire to eight of their own smaller boats and set them sail in the path of the wind which carried them directly to the Spanish fleet setting many of their ships aflame. The Armada vessels sank and amid the smoking roar of cannons and the horrid shrieks and chilling screams of thousands of Spanairds one could see rivers of blood flowing from the decks of the Spanish ships and into the sea. The remnants of the Armada while trying to escape the carnage was nearly devastated by storms in the North Sea.

Only fifty-four of Spains war torn vessles reached the prots of their homeland and of the 27,000 crew members and soldiers of the Armada's original force only 10,000, most of them sick and wounded, survived. The English had lost sixty men and only the eight small ships which they themselves had set fire to. At this crushing defeat Phillip II abandoned the idea of avenging the execution of Mary, Queen of Scots and of ever resinstituting the Roman Church in England again. Following the victory over the Spanish Armada the English people ran wild through the streets, hanging sixty-one catholic priests and forty-nine laymen. Many of the bodies were cut down while the victims were still alive and disemboweled while the limbs were torn from their trunks. Such is the way of "religious wars".

The innate goriness on the part of the whites even towards each other was further manifested in their Euro-American descendants as they heaped untold cruelties and horrors on the Afrikan Slaves often mutilating their bodies and hanging them from trees. This is the way of the white man, this my brothers and sisters you must never forget. That is not to say you must move about in your daily life with a sense of hateful paranoia, this state of mind would be certainly destructive to your natural energy flow and would surface in a host of mental and physical illnesses. Even though it is important for Black People to maintain inner peace, on the other hand we must be prepared to safeguard ourselves and our loved ones by not being lulled into forgetting the real nature of the pale creature we are dealing with. This attitude is essential to the survival and well-being of the Race of which every Black Man, Woman and Child are a part.

Though England's navy won the war with minimal casualties, the ships crews were infected with a violent disease because of the lack of nourishment and supplies due to Elizabeth's extreme frugality in preparation for the war. On some vessels half the crew died or were disabled for life. Still Elizabeth demanded as the most urgent business an accounting of every penny spent before, during and after the battle. When this was done then she inquired as to the state of the crew. The defeat of the Spanish Armada destroyed Spain as a major seapower and brought England to the fore not only as the major sea power in Europe but the number one Protestant Nation in commerical trade. From then on the English became the leading colonizers and slavers in the western world. This growth in sea power is the basis of how the British who descended from one of it not the crudest and most barbaric cultures of old Europe could rise to a place in the world whereas they arrogantly proclaim themselves superior to all others, especially people of color.

Again we must reiterate here that it was the civilizing hand of Afrika by way of the Moors who brought light and culture to Spain, Portugal, Italy and France. Prior to the defeat of the Armada it was the Spanish kings who had been feeding remnants of the Moorish culture to the English, now their power was being eclipsed by the rise of a new and hungry force which was to become the British Empire. Perhaps it would have been better if the Moors had never gone into Europe but they did and anything you see of value in the western world today is a direct or indirect result of the Moorish culture which dominated southern Europe for eight centuries. Now we, their descendants and the progency of Afrikan slaves, must pick up the pieces and extract from the present European dominated world what can be useful to us and continue climbing to the pinnacle of our true station on the Planet Earth. As difficult as this may seem it must be done. It will be done for as the holy utterances of the Honorable Marcus Garvey

84

have so vividly proclaimed "No one knows when the hour of Afrika's reddemption cometh. It is coming. One day like a storm it will be here. When that day comes all Afrika will stand together." Until this occurs my brothers and sisters the Planet Earth will never be at peace.

THE KING JAMES VERSION OF THE BIBLE

James I (1603-1625) of England by whom the King James Version of the Bible was authorized and unto whom it is dedicated is described by his contemporaries as cowardly, dull, narrow-minded, the most learned drunkard in Europe and "the wisest fool in Christendom". His frail being was housed in a dumpy body with spindly legs which bearly held him upright. Often he was seen shuffling from room to room while leaning on the shoulders of a male court favorite whom he would affectionately grab in the buttocks from time to time. Though he was married he had little taste for women but was given to fondling fanciful young men and endlessly falling in love with one cabinet member after another. James I constantly drank to excess and encouraged some court festivities to end in a Bacchannal of bi-sexual intoxication. [148] Because of his thick over-sized tongue when he drank from a cup the contents oozed out from the corners of his mouth. He never changed his clothes until they were worn down to the threads and he is said to have been very unfriendly with water when it came to bathing. This man who had his subjects tortured and sometimes killed for religious descent is the very same one so highly mentioned in the Epistle Dedicatory of the Authorized Version of the English Bible, as "...most dread sovereign which Almight God,...bestowed upon us the people of England, when first he sent your Majesty's Royal Person to rule and reign over us."

This King James Version of the Bible is believed by many to be the unadulterated word of God and the homosexual alcoholic James I to be a saint chosen by the very God himself to authorize its translation into the English language. Though this book became a cornerstone of all future English literature and speech it is not the infallable "word of God" unless of course the Divine Intelligence waited from the time of the creation of earth until the year 1611, when the King James Version was first published, to start speaking to the people of the earth. In the making of this translation, it took forty-six English scholars under the direction of Sir Henry Savile seven years to complete the work and then submit it to William Shakespeare, the dean of English literature, who signified his approval by attaching his signature to the work through a secret literary device. To locate the signature find Psalms 46 in the King James Version of the bible, count forty-six words in from the beginning and you will find the word "shake" then count forty-six words backs from its ending and you will find the word "spear". This denotes William Shakespeare's endorsement of the work carried on by the forty-six English scholars. [149] Besides all this it is the most contradictory version ever translated. For more information on King James read *Afrikan People and European Holidays: A Mental Genocide* Book I, page 6.

In the presentation of this material it is not our intention to attack the basis of anyone's faith or religious belief but rather to set forth the facts as they appear in the annals of recorded history. If we as Black People will be honest with ourselves we will have to admit that most of us really do not know much more about this book (K.J.V. Bible) than the slave master first told us down on the plantation. Although there is much inspiration and wisdom to be garnered from its pages in spite of the corruption and lies written into it by the degenerate translators there is simply no logical way to prove it to be the "Holy Word of God", nevertheless with this as in all things we as a People should use the book in such a way as it can best work to our good and advancement. Though the bible has often been used against us yet with a correct knowledge of self there is so many wonderful ways we can make it work for us. This subject will be discussed in a forthcoming work entitled *The Afrikan Origin of the Bible.*

Now let us continue on our journey as we observe in the next chapter how England acquired some its colonial holdings and the further ecalation of the Afrikan slave trade with the consequent slave uprising carried on by the New Afrikan Revolution.

Chapter Ten

The Growing Empire and The New Afrikan Revolution

CHAPTER TEN

THE GROWING EMPIRE AND
THE NEW AFRIKAN REVOLUTION

PRELUDE

In the past few chapters of this work we have observed how the history of England through the middle ages runs rampant with rivers of blood, the smell of burning human flesh, mutilations, and perpetual war against a background of poverty, unsanitary conditions, pestilence, famine, thievery and murder. These are the morals and values Europeans brought to the New World and took with them to Afrika and other places around the globe where they stole the land and enslaved and colonized the indigenous inhabitants. That is why Afrikans and other people of color in the world today are so out of tune with themselves.

The degenerate, demonic and reprobate ways of the European was brought to their "new world", new for them and "hell for us. In the midst of this hell there continued to develop a revolution which has been going on every since we were first captured and brought to these shores. In fact this revolution started at the slave holding forts set up by Europeans on the West Afrika coast and persisted upon the decks of many a slave ship. In the immortal words of the Honorable Marcus Garvey, "God Almighty created each and every one of us for a place in the world and for the least of us to think that we were created only to be what we are and not what we can make ourselves, is to impute an improper motive to the Creator for creating us. God Almighty created us all to be free. . .to me, a man has no master but God. . . .for man to know himself is for him to feel that for him there is no human master. . . .if he wills to be a real man in possession of the things common to man then he shall be his own sovereign."[161]

Those Afrikans during slavery times who clearly understood these eternal principles consistently fought back through slave revolts which were the beginnings of the New Afrikan revolutionary struggle in the western world. Many of these slave revolts were pitched battles such as those of the Black Maroons who, many times because of their effective armed struggle, forced the British to sign treaties with them as independent New Afrikan nations. This type of rebellion finally culminated in the great Haitian revolution which changed the fate of the world and drove England out of the slave trade.[152] These revolts and rebellions are referred to as the New Afrikan revolution because of the new experiences and formations brought to bear as a result of our deportation here in the west. The terminology New Afrikan means an extension of the Afrikan continent just as the designation New England signifies those colonies as being an extension of the English empire. The continent of Afrika is our mother, the parent stock and we are the children, that is her new born offspring. The designation New Afrikan also applies to the newly resurrected Black man and woman who is being revived to the knowledge that we are descendant from the motherland therefore Afrikans and a seperate and distinct people from Euro-America. To many of our people this concept engenders a new school of thought, thus the New Afrikan political science discipline.

The logical reality set forth here, though very clear to some, is oft times ignored by those Blacks who fancy themselves being American, for many Afrikan people actually believe they are full-fledged equal citizens of this country. In this regard we are reminded of Brother Malcolm's statement that "a cat can have kittens in an oven but that don't make them biscuits." Another good analogy of this principle is the imaginative activity many of us indulged in as children known as making mud pies. Even though as children we would shape the water and dirt mixture to look like a pie and call it peach, apple, sweet potato or some other delectable name it was still mud, not an edible pie. Although mud is a part of the good earth from whence comes the elements for making pies, the mud pies of our childish fantasy did not have the right combination of those elements and therefore not a real pie. To the strong imagination of some children, this might have been a difficult truth to accept but generally a bite from a real piece of pie was all that was needed to establish reality. Thus it should be with those of us who are not children anymore. Though Black people have from time to time, to serve the needs of the white man, been forced into a shadowy shape of an American, we are still Afrikan and can never realistically fit into the Euro-American mold.

Those truly intelligent Black People who embrace this reality and are seeking to create a new life, a new society and a new and better world must understand that this quest can never by fully satisfied until Afrikans everywhere take their rightful place as lords of the earth. Until then there can never ever truly be peace in the world. For the scripture says "When the righteous are in authority, the people rejoice; but when the wicked beareth rule, the people mourn."[153] We submit that two main elements must ever be present in all groupings

88

of Black Folks. 1) We must create and build those independent institutions and formations that will ensure our survival and enhance the quality of life. 2) Most of us must upgrade our present way of looking at things and begin to view all things in light of whether they aid or detract from our collective advancement as a people.

This is the way of all thinking people, for example, the so-called Jews who make up less than 7% of the population in America has more influence over the rest of Euro-America, and many Blacks as well, than any other group because of their dominate control of the mass media systems. Whenever an issue arises that affects the so-called state of Israel, or any other Euro-Jews in the world, these people come to the fore and present their case with such vehemence as to suggest there is nothing else important going on in the world at the time.

In fact, the so-called Jews will not stand still and tolerate any insults to them by anyone at anytime. At the slightest provocation they turn out in full strength to protest any such real or imagined affront to their ethnology. That is why they have established such institutions as the Anti-Defamation League, the Jewish Defense League and many other groups created to defend and lobby their cause in America and around the world. Even if the so-called Jews are caught in the act of wrongdoing their immediate response to their accuser is that they are being persecuted by anti-semitism. Now when Black people stand up and speak on those issues which concerns the oppression and continued enslavement of Afrikans on the Mother continent, here in America, and other places in the world, then we are accused of being paranoid racists in reverse, even by the so-called persecuted Jews themselves. On the other hand, whenever some issue arises, especially pertaining to the so-called state of Israel and their gross misconduct towards the Palestinians or their first-hand involvement in the oppression and extermination of thousands of southern Afrika's indigenous inhabitants, they will in an effort to gain sympathy run a series of television programs dealing with the holocaust of Nazi Germany. They keep the event of Hitler's extermination of 5 million Jews ever before the public as though it was the only atrocity that has ever taken place in the world. Yet very few, if any, of these media monguls say anything about the 100 million-plus Afrikans who died in the middle passage or the millions of Blacks in southern Afrika who cruelly perished under the extermination policies of Cecil Rhodes or the poverty and deprivation, which the so-called Jews are ever ready to feed upon, that Afrikans here and many other places in the world are forced to live in as a result of European colonization and exploitation.

When we as a people raise these issues and recount the cruelty of antebellum slavery, the Jim Crow period, the horrible lynchings, the struggles of the Civil Rights era and the Black Power movement, along with the multitude of other things we have passed through as a eace, the whites and some foolish negroes accuse us of being lost in a time vacuum. They say let bygones be bygones, that which happened in the past happened in the past, let's live for today. But we are the only people who are asked to do this, the Americans have memorialized their struggle with the British Empire, the Russians remember their struggle with Germany, the Chinese never let their people forget the trials and tribulations of their struggle to create a sovereign nationhood. In fact, most everyone else in the world is praised for their liberation but us. New Afrikans are the only people in the world who are told to forget all about what has happened to us and become assimilated and absorbed into the American way of life, of the Marxist way or any other way which suits the needs of Europeans. Therefore we, perhaps more than any other people in the world, must keep ever before ourselves and our posterity the dynamics of the New Afrikan revolution - past, present and future.

Now is keeping with our narrative outline of the British Empire, following is an account of how England acquired some of its colonial holdings. The term 'empire' as used here means a nation which governs, exploits or controls territory outside of its geographical boundries.

CIVIL WAR IN ENGLAND

During the reign of Charles I (1625-1649), England continued to escalate its colonial program. In 1632 Charles awarded George Calvert, Lord Baltimore, a charter to found a colony on the American mainland which became known as Maryland, named so in honor of Charles' Catholic queen, Henrietta Maria. Charles I, who ferverently believed in the divine rights of kings, thought himself above all ordinary law. This attitude kept the monarch in perpetual conflict with Parliament. On one occasion Charles took armed troops to the House of Commons and forcibly closed down the sessions of Parliament. This action eventually led to civil war in England which lasted for seven years and ended in the execution of the king, who was charged with treason and beheaded January 30, 1649

England was then ruled by a Commonwealth government for ten years under the leadership and control of a bloodthirsty Puritan named Oliver Cromwell, dubbed Lord Protector, and for less than one year by his son Richard. For more information on the Puritans, see *Afrikan People and European Holidays: A Mental Genocide*, Book I. The Puritan Parliament of the Commonwealth (1649-1653) seized the properties of the aristocratic landowners to raise funds for replenishing the government treasury, which had been throughly depleted during the civil war. At this time many of the nobility in England fled to America, such as the Washingtons, Madisons and many families of the later patriots. These fugitives from Britain set up tobacco, rice, indigo and other money yielding plantations and purchased thousands of Afrikan slaves to do the back-breaking work on them.

Oliver Cromwell, Lord Protector of England (1653-1658), was the only one of his ten brothers and sisters to survive infancy. In adult life he suffered from depression and hallucinations of death and other mental horrors. Thus he became a strict religious Puritan who thought nothing of massacring the inhabitants of whole villages while praising the name of God. During Cromwell's protectorate, which was a harsh military dictatorship, England made great commercial progress, especially in shipping and the triangular trade. In 1653 the first permanent settlement in the Carolinas was established. The English invaded Jamaica in 1655. The acquisition made Cromwell so happy that he jubilantly discontinued all transactions of business for the rest of the day.[154]

In that same year 1,500 of the Afrikans, who were being brutalized and literally worked to death on the sugar plantations in Jamaica, revolted, fled to the hills and formed guerrilla bands known as Maroons (the Spanish designation for runaway slaves). Of this event John Hope Franklin reports, "When the British took possession of Jamaica in the middle of the 16th century, most of the negro slaves promptly escaped to the mountains and were frequently joined by other fugitives. These runaways, called Maroons, continuously harassed the planters by stealing, trading with slaves, and enticing them to run away. By 1730 these ex-slaves, under Cudjo their powerful leader, had terrorized the whites to such an extent that England was compelled to send out two additional regiments to protect them."[155] Because of the brave struggle waged by these New Afrikan revolutionaries, England was eventually forced to sign treaties with them and to surrender the land they occupied in 1663 and again in 1738.

On September 3, 1658, a paranoid convalescent, Oliver Cromwell, suffering from gout and a host of mental disorders, died and left his son Richard to rule over England. Richard Cromwell lacked the iron character, ambition and fanaticism of his father, this left him at the mercy of the army and Parliament. Unable to hold the Commonwealth together and fatigued by the rigors of political intrigues, Richard resigned the office of Lord Protector May 25, 1659, retired into private life and lived in seclusion until he died in 1712 at age 86, a miracle lifespan for anybody in the English populace at that time.

RESTORATION OF THE MONARCHY

On May 8, 1660, Parliament, along with the popular support of the people of England - who had become sickened by the gloomy and violent rule of the Puritans, invited Charles II, the son of Charles I who had been exiled in France, to come and take possession of the English throne. May 29th of that same year, Charles II re-entered the city of London, amid the tearful rejoicing of tens of thousands of people who fell on their knees and thanked God for his return. This ecstasy soon wore off when the people found Charles II to be a blase, happy go lucky king who cared more for chasing women than attending to affairs of state. On one occasion one of Charles' mistresses threatened to dash out his baby's brains in front of the whole royal court if he did not admit to paternity. Game playing, whoring, drinking and indulging in homosexuality were the favorite pastimes of Charles' court.

During the reign of Charles II (1660-1685), who demanded that his servants approach him on bended knees, English colonial expansion in North America continued to increase. In 1622 Connecticutt Colony was granted a royal charter, Rhode Island was awarded the same in 1663. The British seized Delaware from the Dutch in 1664. North Carolina separated from Virginia and was granted the status of a private company in 1665. New Hampshire became a separate colony from Massachusetts in 1679. The Quaker, William Penn, Jr. - the son of Admiral William Penn who had captured Jamaica for England, was given a patent for East Jersey in 1682. The previous year, 1681, King Charles II, in order to defray a debt of $80,000 owed to William Penn, Sr., gave his son the territory which the sovereign named Penn's Woods (Pennsylvania) in memory of the slave driving Admiral.

In 1663, the same year England took possession of all the Dutch colonies in North America including the state of New York, Parliament passed the second Navigation Act which restricted all English colonial shipping and trading transactions to English ports. The numerous restrictions of this act resulted in the business of smuggling slaves and other forms of secret trade with the West Indian planters and other European colonies such as Santo Domingo (Haiti). This clandestine trade was one of the factors which hastened the beginning of the American Revlution which was mainly fought for control of the profits from the slave trade and sugar plantations rather than the patriotic hocus-pocus so profusely espoused in fantasies about the war of the American Revolution. Eric Williams writes, "It was the wealth accumulated from West Indian trade which more than anything else underlaid the prosperity and civilization of New England and the middle colonies."[156] The reference, West Indian trade, as used here is one and the same with the triangular system of the Afrikan slave trade.

Concerning other events of this same year Walter Rodney reports, ". . . it was no coincidence that when the English struck a new gold coin in 1663, they called it the 'guinea'. . . the guinea was a gold coin at one time current in the United Kingdom. It was first coined in the reign of Charles II, from gold imported from the Guinea coast of west Afrika by a company of merchants trading under charter from the British crown. . ."[157] A guinea coin in those days was worth about $50.00 in today's money.

In the last five years of his reign Charles II became bored with a life of ease and pleasurable self-indulgence and became a serious ruler, devoting himself to administration and politics. This surprised his friends as well as his enemies. On February 2, 1685 he suffered a convulsion and while laying helpless and foaming at the mouth he was, for five days, subjected to the tortures of the crude court physician, who applied a succession of horrid curatives such as bleeding his veins, attaching leeches to his body, raising blisters on his scalp, blowing briers up his nostrils, covering his entire body with pigeon dung and administering a battery of strong enemas. February 7th he called for a Roman Catholic priest, confessed his sins and gladly departed this world and the treatment of his medical attendent. Such, my beloved Black brothers and sisters, is the immutable law of Karma - what goes around, comes around - and so it did for Charles II of England, who had caused so much pain and suffering for Afrikan people.

93

ENGLAND'S GLORIOUS REVOLUTION

Charles II was succeeded by his arrogant and scornful brother James II (1685-1688) who suffered from constant nose bleeds due to the pressures of political maneuvering and government administration, for he, like his older brother, had once given himself over to a life of frivolous debauchery. Now James had become extremely gloomy and warped in his judgment, believing the ultrafeminine Louis XIV, King of France, to be the ideal king. James accepted large sums of money from Louis and worshipfully allowed him to dictate policies for the English government. This action eventually caused James II to lose his throne.

The paranoid sovereign ordered four hundred of his opponents to be hanged and condemned eight hundred others to forced labor in the sugar plantations of the West Indies. In the last years of his reign Lloyd's of London set up business in a small coffee house to insure slave trading voyages. Through its huge profits from slavery and the slave trade it became one of the world's largest and most respected banking and insurance agencies.[168] When James II determined to restore Roman Catholicism as the official religion in England, through the succession of his infant son, all Protestant England, including his daughters Mary and Anne, turned against him and Parliament forced the sovereign to abdicate the throne. This incident is referred to in British history as the Glorious Revolution of 1688. James II was then run out of England and compelled to live the rest of his life exiled in France where he died thirteen years later.

After disposing James II, Parliament invited his daughter, Mary, and her husband, William, Prince of Orange in Holland, to come and rule over England. They accepted on condition that William be the main ruler and Mary be subordinated to him as queen. William III, who reigned in England from 1689-1702, is described as a thin, weak-bodied, frail man with a Roman eagle nose, a crude, impolite "low-Dutch bear" who had atrocious table manners, little regard for women and suffered from constant headaches and repeated fainting spells. He became one of England's most unpopular kings. When William first ascended the throne the merchants of England lent him the sum of ten million dollars in return for favorable foreign policy that would give them a free hand at making big profits from colonial commercial transactions and the Afrikan slave trade.

In 1692 many Afrikans in captivity on the island of Barbados, one of England's sugar planting possessions in the Caribbean, revolted and waged war against the English plantation owners. This is just one of the many rebellions in the long list of the freedom fighting efforts carried forward in the true Glorious Revolution - that is the ever evolving and ongoing struggle of the New Afrikan for land and self-determination.

THE BARBADOS REVOLT

Eric Williams writes, "Barbados was the 'fair jewell' of His Majesty's crown, a little pearl more precious and rare than any the kings of Europe possessed...."[159] During the reign of William III sugar plantations on the little 166 square mile island of Barbados brought more profits to the British crown and merchantile interest than the states of Massachusetts, New Hampshire, Rhode Island, Connecticut, New York and Pennsylvania combined.

The British had laid claim to Barbados in 1605 and secured it from the Portuguese in 1625. The island officially became a crown colony in 1663, during the reign of Charles II, this was England's first possession in the Caribbean. To cultivate sugar crops in Barbados and make possession of the island profitable the English needed gangs of slaves, which they imported from Afrika. By 1692 there were approximately 50,000 slaves and only 20,000 whites but the whites were well armed with the latest weapon technology.

It was on this little "pearl of great price" that some of the harshest seasoning tactics were applied in an effort to break the Afrikan spirit, those methods used to break the slaves were even worse than those used to break a horse or any other beast of the field. John Hope Franklin writes, "One important ingredient in the seasoning process was the overseer's lash...at times the floggings were so severe as to inflict wounds so large that a man's finger could be inserted in them. Another favorite type of punishment was to suspend the slave to a tree by ropes and tie iron weights around his neck and waist. Still another was to crop the slaves' ears and to break the bones of his limbs."[160] The foregoing description is just a small example of the untold horrors inflicted upon the Afrikan slave in order to break his strong and powerful spirit. For more details of the hideous atrocities, read *The Black Jacobins* by C.L.R. James, Chapter One.[161] Though this "...cruel treatment was designed to prevent uprisings and running away, it was imminently unsuccessful." For still, in spite of it, many Afrikans boldly rose in revolt.

Barbados, unlike Jamaica and other sugar islands, was too small to sustain a protracted liberation struggle. The slaves had no interior in which they could flee and maintain Maroon communities as bases of operation from which to wage their guerrilla warfare against the European oppressor. Because of the physical characteristics of the island, the hideouts of the freedom fighters could not withstand the bombardment of British ships. Yet, Blacks bravely rose in successive revolts in 1674, 1692, 1702, and 1816. Because of this tenacious struggle for Black liberation in this area, the whites on the islands of Barbados, Trinidad and St. Thomas lived in constant fear of massacre. We Afrikans, wherever we live in the world today, must never forget this valiant struggle on the part of our Black ancestors which took place on these islands but more importantly we must make certain, in our lifetime, that their struggle was not in vain.

QUEEN ANNE AND THE ASIENTO

The last monarch we will profile in this narrative outline of the British empire in Queen Anne, who reigned 1702-1714, and who, because of her strong Protestant persuasion, had turned on her Catholic father, James II, in 1688. Anne came to the throne of England at the age of 38, upon the death of William III in the year 1702. She is described as a weak, timid, dull-witted woman, unsuitable for the responsibilities of government. Because of the incessant quarrels among her ministers of state and the burdens of rule, her nerves were ever on edge and she was in a constant state of unrest. As a result of her unsteadiness and lack of intellect she left the affairs of government largely in the hands of Parliament and was for many years personally dominated and influenced by her childhood friend and confidant Sarah Jennings, and spouse John Churchill, Duke of Marlborough, ancestor of the war mongering Sir Winston Churchill of 20th century Britain.

Shortly after she ascended the throne Anne saved her degenerate and conniving cousin, Lord Cornbury, from going to prison by making him Governor of colonial New York and New Jersey. While serving in this post Cornbury stated that he wanted "to literally represent the queen", so he was usually seen about town wearing the most elegant and frilly dresses, bonnets and other feminine paraphernalia. The well-groomed transvestite governor could also be observed participating in one of his favorite pastimes, sneaking up behind unsuspecting men and pulling their ears. The queen herself used to make him gifts of gowns and other female attire. Eventually the colonialists complained of his mismanagement of government affairs dubbing him a "peculiar, detestable maggot", whereupon the queen reluctantly removed him from office in December 1708 and he was immediately seized by his creditors and thrown in jail but the queen again came to his aid. Such were the ways of many of England's so-called great men.[162]

Anne, who was very poorly of health, bore children almost yearly but of her seventeen children sixteen died in infancy and the seventeenth at age eleven. August 1, 1714, Queen Anne, her demured spirit further intensified in gloom by so many funerals, died. Thus ending the Stuart dynasty of 100 years upon the throne of England. During her reign England's commercial prosperity and colonial expansion continued in growth. Parliament became the unquestioned supreme power in the country. May 6, 1707 witnessed the signing of the Act of Union which made England, Scotland, and Wales one nation, creating the United Kingdom of Great Britain, as it is so arrogantly called. But the event of most significance to us as Afrikan people is the signing of the Asiento, a trade contract between Spain and England wherein the latter agreed to supply the Spanish colonies in the Americas with a minimum of 144,000 Afrikan slaves over a period of thirty years in exchange for huge profits.

The immediate circumstances leading up to this ominus happening took place in this manner. In 1689, during the reign of William III, a series of conflicts which came to be known as the French and Indian wars broke out between the British and the French colonists in North America. These four wars were fought intermittently from 1689 to 1763. Similar struggles between these two colonial super powers were being engaged concurrently on the European continent. In America they were referred to as the French and Indian wars because of France's heavy dependence on Algonkian Indian allies as the main fighting force. Quite a bit of money and resources was spent by the British government in order to defend the western frontiers in the northern and southern borders of the thirteen colonies against her age old rival France. The French were feverishly engaged in escalating their colonial expansion on the North American mainland and England was determined to abort that plan. This series of antagonisms was four major wars over who was going to control and monopolize the productive machinery and profits from the triangular trade system - the main component being the Afrikan slave trade. It was to this end that Britain and France were simultaneously fighting each other in Europe, India, the Caribbean and North America, while using as many of the indigenous peoples of color for cannon fodder as could safely be used. Eventually England won.

The second war in the series was fought during the reign of Queen Anne and culminated in the peace of Utrecht in Holland, signed April 11, 1713. The most significant aspect of this treaty was the Asiento. This contractual agreement to supply the Spanish colonies with Afrikan slaves had originally been awarded France by the Spanish king and the Pope of Rome and was now surrendered to the British crown, thus sharply curtailing French colonialist expansion and seriously diminishing her foreign possessions. England was jubilant, the long struggle to penetrate the Spanish monopoly in South America and the Caribbean ended in victory for the British.

After this the English forced the Dutch out of the slave trade and became the dominate slave traders in the world. Their empire in America centered in Barbados, Jamaica, other Caribbean islands and the thirteen North American colonies on the mainland. Yearly a total of over 50,000 Black people were kidnapped from our motherland and brought to the shores of the Americas.[163]

THE SEVEN YEARS WAR

The fourth and last French and Indian war was fought from 1754-1763 during the reigns of the English monarchs George II (1727-1760) and George III (1760-1820). It was a struggle between the French and the English which developed from disputes over North American territory in Canada and west of the Ohio River. It was at this time that the infamous George Washington, then a Colonel in the British colonial militia, enters upon the stage of history by attempting to take the French garrison at Fort Duquesnes (Pittsburgh, Pennsylvania). Though "old George" is a hero to white America and renown as the father of their country, to conscious Black people who reside in this land he was just another brutal slave master who held over 300 Afrikans in captivity on his Mount Vernon plantation. This same man, while enjoying all of the amenities and benefits of enforced slave labor, was among those other slave owners and slave traders who in 1776 lambasted King George III for holding the thirteen colonies in bondage.[164] For more information on this subject, read *Afrikan People and European Holidays: A Mental Genocide*, Book I.

Two years after the commencing of the last French and Indian war the Seven Years war burst forth on the European continent and in the colonial territories in India. England and France were brutally and violently waged against each other on these battlefields but according to P.M. Sherlock "The Caribbean became one of the main theatres of

98

war. Each side sent out powerful expeditions that sought to take the enemy's sugar colonies, for imperial policy had changed. The aim was not merely to cripple rival sugar producing colonies but to take them and use them as bargaining counters at the end of the war."[165] Eric Williams says of this life and death struggle between England and France, "The vital issue was not who should be king of this country and who of that, but rather whether Britain or France should dominate the Spanish colonies and be supreme in the Caribbean."[166]

After losing most of her colonial possessions in India, the Caribbean, and portions of North America, France became bankrupt and her vessels of commerce all but disappeared from the sea. On February 10, 1763 a treaty was signed by the archrivals at the Peace of Paris. Of these events Durant writes, "For France the result was enormous losses in colonies and commerce, and a near-bankruptcy that moved her another step towards collapse. For England the results were greater than even her leaders realized: control of the seas, control of the colonial world, the establishment of a great empire, the beginnings of 182 years of acsendency in the world.... Politically the main results of the Seven Years War was the rise of the British Empire."[167]

In that very same year British troops in Pennsylvania, who were losing the war to the Indian forces under the leadership of Chief Pontiac, applied the demonic tactic of biological-warfare. At the command of Sir Jeffery Amherst, who was totally obsessed with his hatred of the red man, clothing and blankets were infested with small pox, which was already taking a heavy toll of the British army, and passed on to the indigenous inhabitants as tokens of peace.[168] Amherst College in the state of Massachusetts is named in honor of this fiendish criminal.

During the period of the fourth French and Indian war the whites in colonial America grew weary of trying to keep Afrikan slave rebellions in check, so they founded a school in the fall of 1760 to help Christianize and mis-educate incoming Blacks, especially the fierce, warlike Coromantees of the Akan people from Ghana but the righteous struggle for freedom, liberation and self-government was relentlessly continued by Afrikan people throughout the western hemisphere.[169] We shall observe some of the dynamic events of that glorious struggle in the following chapter.

Chapter Eleven

The Maroon Wars

CHAPTER ELEVEN

THE MAROON WARS

PRELUDE

W.E.B. Dubois writes, "While the British were fighting obstinately for dynastic disputes in Europe, they were really, in the war of Spanish succession and in the Seven Years War, fighting for profit through world trade and especially the slave trade. In 1713 they gained, by the coveted Treaty of Asiento, the right to monopolize the slave trade from Africa to the Spanish colonies. In that century they beat Holland to her knees and started her economic decline. They overthrew the Portuguese in India, and finally, by the middle of the century, overcame their last rival in India, the French. In the 18th century they raised the slave trade to the greatest single body of trade on earth."[170] Cyril Hamshere states, "Distasteful as it is to present-day thinking, it must be admitted that the West Indian Slave Society worked, and produced the great wealth that helped to finance the revolution in industry which turned Britain into a modern state. The exports of sugar, coffee, cotton and other tropical products helped to finance the defeat of Napoleon, for by 1810 Britain controlled all the Dutch and French colonies except St. Domingue, as well as her own."[171]

Though Britain and the thirteen colonies in America materially prospered from this damnable activity, it was at the sacrifice of great peace and tranquility, for there was the ever present and evolving Pan-Afrikan revolution being carried forward by the Black slave from one extremity of Britain's American empire to the other as well as those valiant and righteous struggles that were being waged by the Afrikan in the Spanish, French, Portuguese and Dutch colonies. Here again we draw from the abundant intellectual wellspring of Dubois, "In the 18th century there were fifteen such revolts: in Portuguese and Dutch South Africa, in the French colonies, in the British possessions, in Cuba and little islands like St. Lucia. There were pitched battles and treaties between the British and the Black Maroons and finally there was a rebellion in Haiti which changed the face of the world and drove England out of the slave trade."[172] We have previously mentioned the Maroon struggle for land and self-determination in the preceding chapter. Now let us examine this particular aspect of the early years of Pan Afrikan revolution in the western hemisphere

The Maroon resistance movement in English controlled territory in the Caribbean began in the days of Oliver Cromwell (1655) and was carried on through the reigns of Charles II, James II, William III, Queen Anne and George I, George II and George III, culminating in the Maroon wars of 1690, 1730-39, and 1795. The following is a brief outline of this valiant struggle for Black Liberation.

"BEFORE I BE A SLAVE, I'LL BE BURIED IN MY GRAVE"

The most noted Maroons are those who escaped from the abominable horrors of the plantations and took refuse in the mountains of Jamaica. The designation Maroon is derived from the Spanish word "cimarron" meaning "untamable, wild, unruly" which is what they considered an Afrikan to be who would not submit to the demonic will of the slave master. To Black freedom fighters in that area it became a term of pride and affection which signified that they intended to never to "controlled" by another. To confirm their feverent commitment to the principle of "liberty or death" the Maroons of Jamaica adopted the cutlass as the symbol of their struggle for land and self-determination.

From 1545 to 1864 there were over fifty Maroon communities scattered throughout the swamps and mountain forest of the American colonies in such places as South and North Carolina, Virginia, Louisiana, Florida, Georgia, Mississippi, Alabama, Guadalupe, Cuba, Jamaica, Haiti and Brazil, to name a few. Many of these Maroons fought on the side of the Red man against the European colonial usurpers. Jamaica's Maroon settlements headed this list because its wild mountain terrain provided an ideal sanctuary for runaway slaves. Descendants of these fascinating communities remained steadfast and continued to grow from generation to generation while wreaking havoc on the European settler colonies.

Because of the many Maroon rebellions, England nearly lost Jamaica as a colonial possession. White plantation owners on the island of Jamaica lived in constant fear of the threat of collective slave rebellion for they were ever conscious of the fact that high up in the Blue Mountains were the well organized and disciplined fighting forces of Maroon guerrilla bands. In 1673 when 300 Afrikans slaves arose in revolt, killed their master and thirteen other whites, the planters were virtually thrown into a state of dismay and panic. This type of revolt occurred throughout all the American colonies with recurrent frequency.

On the island of Jamaica each dawn revealed the Maroon visitation of the night before. Descending the mountains in swift night raids the guerrilla bands, armed with carefully planned information received from the slaves who were involved in their intricate intelligence operaion carried on from plantation to plantation, would replenish their food and ammunition by raiding crops, livestock and firearms. Often these fierce warriors would kill the slave masters and overseers and assist the slaves in escaping to the hills. Many a tropical night sky was brilliantly lighted by the highly efficient fighting tactic of guerrilla warfare, often trapping the British forces in ambush after ambush, then mysteriously vanishing into the woods as though they had never been present. This left the whites in a state of dread and consternation.

To really appreciate the Maroon method of warfare it must be remembered that these men were for the most part armed with weapons that were considered antiquated against Great Britain, the acknowledged "mistress of the seas", whose empire at that time covered approximately one-fourth of the then known world. These relentless warriors were the originators of guerrilla warfare and camouflage ambush techniques in the western hemisphere and were past masters of their creation.[173]

THE FIRST MAROON WAR

In 1655 the English took Jamaica from Spain, at the time of this acquisition the mountains were already teeming with some 1,500 or more runaway slaves - whose numbers were being swelled daily be a continuous stream of Afrikans seeking freedom. These Maroons continued the struggle against British troops under the leadership of a Black man named Juan Dubolo, whom the Spaniards referred to as Juan de Bolas. The military skill and courage of these Afrikans laid the foundation for the Maroon wars that were to follow in the wake of their dynamic strike for liberty.

The Blacks could probably have taken complete control of the island had it not been for the fierce tribalism which often divided them. On some occasions certain Afrikans from different geographical locations gave into their old tribal rivalries and refused to fight side by side with each other. From this, we the Afrikans who strive for liberation today, must learn a great lesson and determine among ourselves that we shall not repeat this destructive mistake again. This is difficult but it must be done if we are to win the war. Herein lies one of our main weaknesses as a people. This sickness must be and by the grace of Almighty God it will be healed. Even if the Creator has to turn every force in the world against us to force us to join unto our own. In 1660, largely due to this demoralizing tribalism, Colonel Dubolo and about 150 of his soldiers surrendered to the English in exchange for pardon, land and freedom. But most of the Maroons stayed in the mountains and continued to wage guerrilla war.

At the outset of the reign of James II in 1685, 150 slaves revolted in Jamaica and took to the hills, in 1690 some 400 rose up in arms and joined the Maroons in the Blue Mountains. Between 1663 and the treaty agreement of 1739 there were at least ten major slave revolts occurring within the context of the ongoing war between the Maroons and Britain. In 1730 the English launched an intensified military campaign agains the Maroons with the intended purpose of annihilating their guerrilla bands and obliterating their communities. British regiments were transported to the island from various locations in the empire and a bounty of $28.00 was offered for each Maroon's head delivered. This all out offensive is recorded in British annals as the first Maroon war. The result was Britain's formal recognition of Maroon independence in the Treaty of 1739, which we will discuss later in this chapter.

GENERAL CUDJOE AND HIS AKAN CADRE

During the revolt of 1690 there emerged a bold, strong, resourceful leader of the Blue Mountain Maroons, a slave from the Coromantee tribe of Ghana named Cudjoe. General Cudjoe is described as a "short, stocky, powerfully built man with a humped back."[174] He was a remarkably skilled technician of guerrilla warfare who spearheaded the Maroon revolutionary movement through fifty years of intensive struggle. This warrior chieftain was a supreme tactician who organized and systematized the Maroon army into a highly sophisticated fighting machine. Colonel C.L.G. Harris respectfully says of him, "As the first successful revolutionary in the New World -- and he had many followers and imitators -- General Cudjoe of the Maroons lit the brightest torch of true freedom for all the New World."[175]

Though a brilliant military commander and administrator of the highest caliber, he was sometimes unpredictable and irrational and could be ruthless, even brutal to his own people. Yet, at times he was ambivalent in his dealings with whites and all to easily seduced by their call for peace and friendship. For this ex-slave, mighty giant that he was, suffered from the mental disorder of extreme contradictions which is so often prevalent in a mind which has once been disarranged by its former oppressor. Still, General Cudjoe's commitment to combat the brute force of the slave masters and establish independence for his Maroon followers was impeccable. Through rivers of blood, over jagged mountains and through myriad dangers untold, he led he forces to victory after victory and lived to be well over eighty years of age after the signing of the Treaty of 1739.

Cudjoe and most of his cadre were Akan people from the Coromantee tribe of Ghana. The Coromantee were a strong and highly developed militaristic group of Afrikans superbly proficient in jungle warfare. Generally they had a fierce intolerrance to slavery which they had never known prior to their captivity in the Americas. The Coromantee provided most of the leaders in the rebellions and insurrections among the slaves in Jamaica. Here is a partial listing of Jamaican Maroon leaders. General Cudjoe; his brother, Accompong, named in honor of Akjanpong, the Akan designation for Creator of heaven and earth; another brother, Johnny; and his formidable and brilliant sister, Nanny. The leaders of the Maroons on the windward part of the island were Captains Quaco, Cuffee and Kishee, to name a few.

THE MAROON TREATY OF 1739

After nearly ten years of intensified warfare with the Maroons, the English were forced to sue for peace. Because of the superiority in guerrilla warfare which had been consistently demonstrated for over three-quarters of a century by the New Afrikan freedom fighters on the island of Jamaica, the British had no alternative but to ask the Maroons, whom they had been unable to defeat and subdue, to make peace. On March 1, 1739 diplomacy succeeded where brute force had failed and the Maroons were declared free and independent forever.

The terms of the treaty granted them 2,500 acres of land and the status of a Maroon state within the Jamaica colony - with the freedom to plant, harvest and sell any crop but sugar. In return Trelawny, British governor on the island at that time, required them to return all fugitive slaves after the date set forth in the treaty in exchange for monetary compensation, to aid in the suppression of future slave revolts, receive and maintain at least two white superintendents in the Maroon territory and come to the defense of the island in times of foreign invasion. Hamshere says, "It is strange that the Maroons accepted these conditions but they were exhausted and their women and children were near starvation."[176] In the book *Maroon*

Societies Richard Price records, "Following the treaties, these same Jamaican Maroons bought, sold and owned substantial numbers of slaves, hunted new runaways for a price, managed to gain the hatred of much of the slave population, and in many respects may have deserved their common post-treaty nickname, the 'king's niggers.'"[177]

This contradictory behavior on the part of the Maroons was created by the bizarre circumstances and strangeness of the slavery phenomenon which engendered the psychological schizophrenia or warring conflicts and confusion within the mind and spirit of what was originally a free and independent people. We are not here seeking to overlook or excuse this imbalanced behavior but rather to learn from and transcend it. We must somehow come to understand the real meanings of these happenings and extract from them the object lessons that will make us stronger, wiser and better Afrikans today. The mental genocide, physical and spiritual abuses of chattel bondage affected even the strongest-willed Blacks. During that period, Caribbean islands like Jamaica were main centers of the "seasoning" process, where the slave was beaten, tortured and brainwashed into dehumanized submission so that even in the case of some of the freedom fighting slaves who warred to the death for self-determination and independence, there was yet a great deal of confusion of mind and behavior.

There are those who would discount the real significance of the Maroon wars on the basis of their acceptance of the terms of the treaty. But to do this would be unwise for it would blot out a very important feature of the New Afrikan revolution. Though I do not even pretend to fully comprehend or am I disposed to excuse the Maroon's contradictory behavior, these are the thoughts which come to mind in regards to this issue. No one really knows the full impact of slavery on the psyche and its total distortion of the otherwise normal and logical function of the mind of the enslaved. It must be remembered that the white slave master systematically stole our minds and a portion of our souls, as well as our bodies. The seasoning method used in the island was designed to strip the Afrikan of all his humanity and loyalty to self and kind. So thoroughly was the job done that even in the great Black leaders of the current 20th century we still view contradictions in our most dedicated freedom fighters, yet we must be wise enough not to dismiss all the wonderful and good things done for the race by such magnificent personages as the Honorable Marcus Garvey, the Honorable Drew Ali, the Honorable Elijah Muhammad, Malcolm X, Dr. Martin Luther King, Jr., and a host of others too numerous to mention here. These mighty men and women gave so completely of themselves to advance the race further and further towards our eventual goal of nationhood and Black liberation. It is in the holy deeds of these saints that we must glory and strengthen ourselves as a people. As regards to their mistakes and contradictions, we must move to a higher plateau in our continuing struggle by learning from and resolving never to repeat them again. This is the legacy of our time, the good deeds of our ancestors are our guideposts to freedom, their mistakes and contradictions are the warning signs of what lies ahead. Learn from them and let us move ever forward in the principle of Pamoja Tutashinda (We will win together) that all the world may see that we are One.

From the Maroon contradiction we must assuredly learn our lesson so that we can never be fragmented against each other again as has been so recently demonstrated in the succumbing of many of our leaders and Black organizations to the ego and personal gratification manipulations of the United States Government's Cointelpro Offensive. Here is where the supreme power of discipline comes in. Individual Blacks and/or organizations must come to embrace the concept of the New Afrikan Creed which speaks of "... fashioning victory in concert with my brothers and sisters."[178] This was the principle taught by our High Culture Systems of the ancient world, the divine law of the collective which was basic to the Afrikan's nature and behavioral manifestations prior to captivity.

Those of us who are serious students of human nature understand that the first law of the individual is the law of self-preservation and self-aggrandizement. This is the law of the jungle, the law of the caveman, the law of the untamed and underdeveloped spirit. The first law of the community as taught by our Ancient High Culture System is Umoja (unity, oneness), based on the principle of collective participation and cooperative gain. This is the basic difference between a civilized and an uncivilized society. The law of the collective places man above the level of the lower animals. The law of the individual puts him on the level of the dog-eat-dog behavioral patterns of the beast of the field. This is the realm to which many Afrikans and their societies were reduced after our enslavement and perpetual bondage. Remnants of this degeneration of the high Afrikan collective ideal and consciousness are still evident in Black communities today. This is perhaps our greatest weakness and is starkly manifested in our extreme tribalism, egotism, and organizational exclusivity. This must be overcome if we are to rise to the position of power to which the race is destined. Truly, as a people, we have far more in common than we have differences. Thus we should ever seek that ground of commonality in our individual and organizational relationships with each other, thereby maximizing our efforts to constructively function together for the total good of the whole. In the words of the Honorable Marcus Garvey our attitude must be One Aim, One God, One Destiny.

THE SECOND MAROON WAR

Not all Maroons, especially those Blacks who were still on the plantation, were in agreement with the treaty. Slave uprisings and revolts continued to be prevalent in Jamaica. In 1760 over 1,000 Afrikans rose in rebellion under the leadership of a brother named Tackey and killed sixty whites, once again striking terror in the hearts of the planters. In 1765 Black people on seventeen plantations arose and struck for freedom, the very next year some Coromantee slaves revolted. In 1776, the year of the signing of the United States Declaration of Independence, several hundred slaves rose in insurrection on two separate parts of the island. In 1795 the second war between the Maroons and the British colonial government in Jamaica erupted. This was lasted from July to December of that year. Over 1,500 British troops and 3,000 militia were mustered in an effort to subdue the Maroons of Cudjoe's settlement, then called Trelawny Town, but they failed. Finally the English imported bloodhounds from Cuba and the Maroons were forced to surrender and return to their designated bounderies as defined in accordance with the treaty of 1739. Immediately following this event Coromantee Blacks, who were enlisted in the colonial government's West India regiment, mutinied and took to the hills. Their leader was called Chamba. In 1815 Ibo slaves, captures from Nigeria, laid plans for a slave revolt, there were at least three other such conspiracies on the island between 1823 and 1824. In 1831 occurred the largest slave uprising in Jamaican history. Over 20,000 Afrikans, led by Daddy Sharp, rose in rebellion against the British colonial government causing the English to step up their efforts in abolishing slavery in the declining sugar islands of the Caribbean.[179]

This ongoing revlutionary activity on the part of the Blacks cost the British government a great deal of money, lives and resources, not the mention the taxing mental strain of the ever present threat of recurring slave insurrections. The productivity of the plantations was seriously hampered for a time and travel into the interior of Jamaica was dangerous. During the first Maroon war alone, the British spent over 700,000 dollars, quite a sum in those day. P.M.S. Sherlock writes,

"For the first time in the history of the Americas a metropolitan power was forced to recognize the rights of their subjects to independence. This happened a half a century before the North Americans gained their independence, and seventy years ahead of the Blacks of Haiti. This is essence is the meaning of the Treaty of 1739 which brought an end to the first Maroon war."[180] In 1865 there was an insurrection of Afrikans in the Morant Bay area under the leadership of Paul Bogle. Eventually on August 6, 1962 Jamaica became the first British territory in the Caribbean to gain national independence.

ROLE CALL OF AFRIKAN FREEDOM FIGHTERS IN COLONIAL TIMES

The widespread passion for freedom among the slaves and the will to struggle for it created a long list of Black freedom fighters from this period. Following is a few of them. On the island of Hispaniola in 1545, an Afrikan with the slave name of Diego de Campo led a large Maroon community of approximately 7,000. His guerrilla band defeated many Spanish troops sent against them, burned down sugar mills (the main colonial product) and set many slaves free. This mights warrior chieftain was feared by the whites throughout the island and they offered to sue for peace. In 1650 Afrikans of northeastern Brazil revolted and proclaimed themselves the independent republic of Palmares, named in honor of the abundance of palm trees in the region of their liberated territory which provided them with food and other products they used in trade with the Red man and some of the coastal settlements. This Black republic endured from 1650 to 1697. In 1654 the Portuguese retook northeast Brazil from the Dutch and attempted to take Palmares from the Afrikan. After failing at this some twenty-five times they were forced to recognize the independence of this New Afrikan republic. The most outstanding head of state in the government of Palmares was a brilliant administrator and brave warrior named Zumbi. Afrikans in the Dutch held South American colony of Surinam, Guiana fought for their liberty in a thirty-six year war. The Dutch, unable to subdue the freedom fighters by force, sued for peace and concluded an amicable treaty in 1761 with Captain Adoe, leader of the revolutionary forces whom the Dutch called Bush Negroes. Of course we can never forget the Santo Domingo revolution of 1791 to 1803 which evolved into the total abolition of slavery there and the existence of the first independent Black Nation in the western hemisphere.

As we reflect on this period of Afrikan history names, such as Toussaint and Dessalines of Haiti, Dagga of Trinidad, Adoe of Surinam, Cudjoe, Nanny, Accompomg, Dubolo, Tackey, Paul Bogle, Chamba and Daddy Sharp of Jamaica, Zumbi of Palmares, Diego de Campo of Hispaniola, Gabriel Prosser, Denmark Vesey, Nat Turner and Harriet Tubman of the United States and a host of others too numerous to mention here, flash across the consciousness in brilliant succession, a legacy more precious than gold, more vital to us than all the material treasures of the world today, for in the good acts of these saints - though they were not perfect - we behold the various embodiments and manifestations of the true Afrikan spirit, the spirit of excellence and power.

In the preceding discussions we have mentioned just a minute few of the incalculable examples of the New Afrikan revolution and the ever present struggle for land and self-determination which was then, even as now, carried on throughout the Americas, culminating in the founding of many independent Black Nations in the western hemisphere and the recent creation of the Provisional Government of the Republic of New Afrika, March 31, 1968. This subject will be set forth in more detail in a forthcoming work entitled *The Rape of Afrika and the Settling of the New World*.

The middle to the latter part of the 18th century marked one of the greatest periods of New Afrikan revolutionary activity. At the same time that the western sector of the British empire was being plagued by the constant revolt of the ongoing Black Liberation struggle, she became embroiled in a controversy with the thirteen colonies of North America which led to a full-scaled revolutionary war on the part of her wayward child. This conflict led to the creation of the United States of America. We will now proceed to discuss this event and its true relationship to Afrikan people in the succeeding and final chapter of this book.

Chapter Twelve

The American Revolution: A Sham

CHAPTER TWELVE

THE AMERICAN REVOLUTION
PRELUDE

In this chapter we will expose some of the lies which have been and are now being told to you and your children about the American Revolution. Those of us who are observant and aware know that the Euro-American must define and lie about the Black man's history in order to keep the facade of his superiority intact. When the truth of the matter is, were it not for Black people, America would still be a colonial subject of the British crown. Through the digging out of truth by earnest men we are learning that the mighty institutions of Europe and America are not only built off Black backs but also off Black facts, that is the original Afrikan knowledge and science brought to Europe and America by the Black man.

The major events leading up to the American Revolution are rooted in the 1) commercial revolution, 2) agricultural revolution and 3) industrial revolution of 18th century Europe. In previous chapters we have shown how the foundations of Moorish science laid the basis for these advances, especially in the areas of agriculture, and how these technical and commercial revolutions were made possible by the hugh profits from slave labor and the slave trade.

Just as in the study of the Protestant Reformation discussed in Book I of this series through our overview of the American Revolutionary war we are still observing a struggle between European nationlists. The British were involved in a struggle European nationalists. The British were involved in a struggle with the French on the European continent, India, the Caribbean Islands and North America. Later on the 13 colonies, because of the heavy tariffs and restrictions placed on the slave trade and its subsidizers by the parent government, began fighting for their independence from the British empire, this is the real essence and meaning of the American Revolution.

In this chapter we are greatly dependent upon and heavily indebted to the works of Joel A. Rogers, one of the foremost pioneers in the field of Afrikan history. Some may perhaps wonder why I am prone to draw so often from this man's works. My reply is few historians can match the profuseness of his documentation, in fact, many of the sources Rogers quoted are not even in print today and those in existence are in rare book sections of certain libraries and private collections. Oh that expense and sacrifice must have been endured by this brother in laying the groundwork for those of us who follow in his scholarly footsteps. For closer look at Professor J.A. Rogers and his priceless contribution to this field see *Afrikan People and European Holidays: A Mental Genocide*, Book I, pages 10-11.

THE SUGAR ACT: DON'T MESS WITH MY MOLASSES

"The Peace of Paris had just ended Britain's long war with France and Spain and she was badly in need of revenue to pay her huge national debt. America, at peace, had been growing more and more profitable...the English press and Parliament demanded that America be made to bear the burden. The Molasses Act, now called the Sugar Act, was revived. Britain sent out twenty-seven warships to patrol the New England coast and soldiers and revenue agents to enforce the act. American shipping and general commerce at once felt the effect. Providence and Medford, chief slave-ports, suffered heavily. So did other cities as far south as Charleston. One merchant wrote, 'what are the people of England going to do with us? Nothing but ruin seems to hang over our heads'."[181]

In 1733 the British Parliament passed a bill imposing high taxes on molasses and sugar imported into the thirteen colonies from their French and Spanish competitors in the sugar islands of the Caribbean. The purpose of this piece of legislation was to give the British a tota. monopoly over the West Indian with her North American colonies. This bill was known as the Molasses Act. The colonists, who needed the molasses for making rum to be used in exchange for slaves on the West Afrikan coast, generally ignored it. The Molasses Act also prohibited American exports to the Caribben Islands controlled by foreign powers other than Britain. The thirteen colonies, especially New England, were heavily dependent on the West Indian trade for sustenance and economic prosperity. The sugar plantation industries in turn were dependent on the North America colonies to supply the ammunition and staples needed to feed themselves and control the large slave labor force used to work the sugar, tobacco and indigo estates on the Islands.

Another source of antagonism between England and the thirteen colonies arose when the British government's proclamation of October 7, 1763 prohibited colonial settlements west of the Appalachian Mountains. This was an effort, on the part of the home government, to slow down the westward expansion of the colonies in North America and to keep the Euro-Americans in the thirteen colonies on the seacoast from making big profits through supplying manufactured goods to the invaders who settled beyond the mountains. The British rescued these lands for the Red Man hoping to tighten their grip on the colonists and keep them economically dependent on the home government. Because it would interfere with the confiscation of large tracts of land

and the making of immense profits, the Americans viewed these limits stipulated by the proclamation as unjust and illegal. And they resisted it.

In that same year Parliament decided to maintain a standing army of British troops in North America. To support and maintain this army the legislators in London looked to the tax revenues from colonial trade and navigation. Therefore they revived the Molasses Act of 1733 and in 1764 passed the Sugar Act with full intentions of strictly enforcing it. The Euro-American businessmen, envisioning their slave based commercial interests in ruins, became infuriated almost of the point of rebellion so the British government reduced the duty to a minimum in 1766. The Molasses and the Sugar Act which was directly linked to the Afrikan slave trade were the main contributing factors to the beginnings of revolutionary activity in the thirteen colonies.

THE STAMP ACT CAUSES RIOTS IN THE STREET

"Rum and slave trading are not glamorous and patriotic items therefore most popular historians and text-books omit them. Instead stress is laid on the Stamp Act which came into being to make up for the loss of revenue on the reduction of the taxes on sugar and molasses. The Stamp Act, long used in England forced America to use stamped paper on all legal documents. It also taxed newspapers, pamphlets, magazines, advertisements, almanacs, playing cards and dice."[182]

March 1765 Parliament passed the Stamp Act in an attempt to make up for the dwindling revenues from the Sugar Act. The Molasses and Sugar Acts directly involved the slave merchants and other commerical interest. The general Euro-American colonial populace of approximately 2 million had little or no concern for it but the Stamp Act and the tax on tea and other household commodities affected the masses and thus became the rallying point for stirring up general discontent with the home government. This flammatory stituation was skillfully manipulated, by the slave mongers of the New England colonies and the plantation magnates in the South, to the fever pitch of the cry for independence from Britain in 1776. The commoners were not really that concerned about the issues but the merchants and plantation owners continued to fan the flame until it erupted into a full-scale revolution from which the land barons and merchants benefited the most.

The Stamp Act was as unpopular with the planters and merchants of the Caribbean Islands as it was with those on the North American mainland. Yet the discontent of the thirteen colonies was manifested through rallying the masses to a frenzy whereupon they refused to allow the stamps to be sold and publically burned them in the streets, amid shouts of liberty and the resisting chants of "taxation without representatioin is tyranny." The term representation is used here in reference to the fact that there were no mainland American colonial representatives in the British Parliament. Faced with the prospects of a general uprising the lawmakers in London repealed the Stamp Act in 1776, then immediately passed the Declaratory Act which was little more than a "wolf ticket" claiming full British authority over the thirteen colonies.

A QUESTION OF ECONOMICS: NOTHING PERSONAL, JUST BUSINESS

"It was the wealth accumulated from West Indian trade which more than anything else underlay the prosperity and civilization of New England and the middle colonies... the population and wealth of England after slumbering for seven-hundred years began to develop itself under the influence of slave-acquired capital. How dare American, colonials, to become their rivals demanded the English. Were not the colonies founded for the benefit of the mother-country? To make it still worse, the Americans with their trade were helping to develop the colonies of their great rival, France."[183]

Even during the French and Indian war of 1754-1763 the North American colonists continued to trade with French sugar islands in the Caribbean. The West Indian colonies needed food and other commodities supplied by the thirteen colonies. Because all the land suitable for planting on the islands was taken up in the growing of very profitable cash crops such as sugar cane, indigo and coffee. Therefore in the estimation of the planters they could not afford the luxury of using land and labor for cattle grazing and growing food. On the mainland colonies, particularly New England, these staples were produced in surplus abundance, so the North American colonists exchanged such commodities with any planters who would trade with them for molasses, sugar, and gold in return. The North-American colonies became the bread basket for the various slave-labor hell holes of colonial possessions in the Caribbean. This, England would not tolerate and the struggle was on. As Eric Williams says, "Disseverance of the United States from the British Empire, viewed as a mere question of commerce...."[184]

AFRIKAN SLAVE TRADE AND THE AMERICAN REVOLUTION

"The War of the American Revolution really began in rivalry over the

Afrikan slave-trade. The American colonies, principally the New England ones, was taking it away from the mother-country principally by using rum as barter for slaves, ivory, gold and other products...in plain language, therefore, it was the profit from the sale of Afrikans and the wealth they produced that was the underlying cause of the revolution. In short, had there been no Africa, the United States might still be attached to Britain...thus the wealth gained from the sale of Afrikans and their labor not only laid the foundation of America's commerce but the attempt to deprive here of the benefit of the slave trade was the most direct cause of the revolution."[185]

A quarrel over the Afrikan slave trade and its attendant industries formed the basis for the American Revolution. The Euro-American colonies had become arrogant and were referred to by the British officials as "dogs and their wives bitches."[186] Now the fact that they had Black slaves to work the plantations and pull big profits for the landowners caused the ex-convict Euro-American to become conceited and rebellious to the authority of the parent government which had first exported them here. This unreasonable arrogance on the part of Euro-American whites has been carried on into recent times. That is why he is labeled by the rest of the world as the "ugly American."

In early Henry Fonda movies, I have heard him say so matter of factly "free, white and twenty-one." In the movies and television shows of today the same attitude prevails but it is done in a much more sophisticated manner. The "mammies" are no longer in the visual media of current films, but the idea is put across very subtly, as can be seen in the latest 'Come Back to Jamaica' commercials. The conditioning process is also reinforced by the fact that Black actors and actresses can only get parts as supportive personnel to lesser white persons, i.e., Billy Dee Williams and Sylvester Stallone, Richard Pryor and Gene Wilder and Lavar Burton playing a role in a Steve McQueen movie that was originally written for a dog. In a new movie release—The Toy, Richard Pryor allows Jackie Gleason's people to put money into his hand and buy him as a plaything for the white man's son. These are just a few of the media images that are created and projected with the design of keeping Black people in the United States, particularly Black youth in a mental state of low self-esteem. The object is to program us to a servile status, to dilute the innate desire in the race to rise up and create a world of their own. That is why black liberation teachers of today are working so hard to break the chains of our minds and free us from America's modern day sophisticated and subtle mind-conditioning mechanisms.

As regards the Afrikan slave trade and the American Revolution Rogers says, "it is impossible to over-estimate the impact of the

Afrikan and the Afro-American on the United States from 1512 to 1865." This is not something we as a people should necessarily be proud of but it is a fact we must never forget. If we could build a nation for them, why can we not now build one for ourselves? I am sure that if you sufficiently meditate on this question you will be brought to the "light of understanding." Remember "the Creator has a Master Plan" for the Black man.

THE STATE OF THE RACE DURING THE AMERICAN REVOLUTION

"Patrick Henry declared that while he would not and could not justify slavery, he found Negroes a necessity. 'I am drawn along', he said, 'by the general inconvenience of living without them.' In his address to the Virginia Convention, June 24, 1788 he deplored 'the necessity of holding his fellow-men in bondage' but that 'their manumission is incompatible with the facilities of the country.' Thomas Jefferson and other...slave holders said much the same."[187]

The American Revolution is in essence white folks history, not ours, we just happened to be here. In most cases, as a result of our captivity and enslavement and in some cases, as the saying goes in Hollywood, we were considered to be extras, in the supporting cast. If you had asked most of the thinking Black people in the colonies during the American Revolution and the War of 1812, they would have told you that these events meant nothing for them, save another opportunity to take advantage of the confusion which tends to accompany warfare, by making a strike for their own freedom. Surely nothing concerning the landmarks of American history held anything for the black slave to celebrate except his struggle for independence. In 1775 a grand plot conspired by the Afrikan and the Indian to cast off their overlords was discovered in the New York colonies. Unnerved by this, local officials gave the order to shoot on sight any Black man or Red man out after dark and the possession of firearms by the same was to be punished with no less than the death penalty. At this time many slaves ran away and joined the Indians, others offered their services to the British who supplied them with arms, these slaves harassed their masters, slaughtered them and their families and conducted their armed attacks on their former masters with such efficiency the exasperated American Colonists accused the British of starting "a race war." The British had promised the Black man his freedom, consequently many Afrikans fought on the side of the Redcoats and won many battles for them.

During the 18th century enslavement of Black people was a deeply and firmly rooted institutional way of life in the American

115

colonies, particularly in the South. And though in some instances the emotional bond between the slave and his master was often very strong yet in the case of the thinking slave this was not sufficient. For when the Black slave began to realize his own self-worth and to understand that he was sent to planet Earth to serve God's will and not to be the servant of another or to be used like a good dog, or horse, or cow. He then set out to rebel against his slave master and this he did often during the course of the American Revolutionary war. Brother Malcolm once reminded us that though some Black people think they came here on the Mayflower we were in actuality brought to these shores as livestock and sold on the slave market like a horse, or a cow, or a chicken. In fact white folks were passing Black people around as if they were old clothes, on one occasion General Braddock, after he had been fatally wounded in a fight, bequeathed his bodyguard, a Black slave named Bishop, to George Washington as a gift.

Though there were some free Black men like Paul Cuffee (1759-1817) who became a rich philanthropist and did much for the upgrading of the race. And those few token Blacks such as Benjamin Bannaker (1731-1806) an astronomer, mathematician, surveyor, builder and virtual genius who laid out the plans for the District of Columbia, that is why conscious Afrikans refer to this metropolis as Bannaker City. There was still the general misuse and abuse of Black skilled labor and talent by the slave masters who held the legal title to their persons. The slave owner would hire out the skilled and artistic crafts of the slave and receive wages of same unto his own pocket. This same principle applies on the job market in America today, Black people are still being "hired out", the employer makes big profits and a small fraction of this is your salary. I have even witnessed on one occasion in a white suburban neighborhood in Richard Allen City (Philadelphia), one white woman talking over her backyard fence to another and saying "Do you want this girl tomorrow or would you rather I keep her until next week"in reference to a fully grown Black woman who was standing silently nearby. That is why it is so necessary for us as a people to create our own economic and commercial institutions so that we may fairly employ as many of our people as possible. This was the program presented to use by the Honorable Marcus Garvey, the Honorable Elijah Muhammad and many other great teachers who has been raised in our midst.

In light of this some will raise the issue that there were white indentured who were being exploited during the days of the American Revolution also. This is true but the descendants of those white indentured servants are today's recipients of the life-giving and sustaining American institutions which were created for them as a race. All

116

around them, everyday, in everyway they see evidences of their kind as overlords and rulers in this land. Thus every white can in some way identify with and thereby apply himself to the pursuit of the American dream. But on the other hand, for black folks in this country there is a gross identity problem, rooted in the reality that on every turn we see evidences of a power system which has not been created to our best interest. Therefore it becomes self-evident "...that the fundamental reason our oppression continues is that we, as a people, lack the power to control our lives...and that the fundamental way to gain that power and end oppression, is to build a sovereign Black nation."[188] Though others may have the luxury to live in some degree of fantasy, we cannot, Afrikan people must always deal in truth, no matter how cold or harsh that truth may be. Then we must rise to the occasion and transform that truth into a new and better reality, for we are not compelled by any force of nature to accept present transient, un-pleasant conditions as final. In the words of the Honorable Marcus ·Garvey, Up You Mighty, You Can Accomplish What You Will.

Those Black People who embrace this country's so-called democracy and the American way, a nebulous concept which very few can clearly define, are merely chasing a dream that even the average white person cannot have. The little man is stuck with patriotism, the capitalists enjoy the fruits of international investments. The attitude of the huge corporations and the big money people is, Capital has a life of its own, therefore they will follow it wherever it goes. The captialist only indulges in patriotism when he wants the masses to fight and protect something that is his or that is valuable to him. Thus is was during the days of the American Revolutionary War. The wage earners and the landless could not vote, hence, the "hypocrisy". The "all men are created equal" clause of the United States Declaration of Independence meant in actuality — you are equal if you are white and have some land. Even in the electoral voting system in this country today the masses of the people are not truly represented, most Senators are either rich men or controlled by rich men. Thus the wisdom of the Honorable Elijah Muhammad when he taught us that "land is the basic fundamental of wealth". For example, note the respect given to Nigerian political leaders and other peoples of color who have land and wealth. This respect is not accorded because America loves or neces-sarily likes them but rather because they have something which America wants and needs, for instance, Nigeria is her third largest importer of oil.

The United States government while yet boasting of her two centuries of independence from the British Empire still overtly, covertly and aggressively fights against the independence movement and the quest for sovereignty of her ex-slaves here in America. Her vicious attacks on the Republic of New Afrika and the undermining of the Nation of Islam are just two prime examples of Euro-America's unwillingness to see the Black man with something he can call his own. Recently much has been espoused by one of this country's former heads of state about human Rights, the rights of an individual to change governments and the right to self-determination for those who are being treated unfairly by the governmental structures in which they reside. These basic principles are embodied in the United Nation's Resolution of 1514 and 1451. Yet America has shown no intent to recognize the legitimate struggle for land and self-determination on the part of the Blacks in this country. Thus we see my beloved Black brothers and sisters that there has been little change in the state of the race in terms of true "freedom, justice and equality" for the Black man in this country from the days of the American Revolution until now.

CRISPUS ATTUCKS: MARTYR FOR AN UNWORTHY CAUSE

"One Negro, Crispus Attucks, probably an escaped slave, took the lead in the event that led most directly to the war of the revolution, and through that to American independence. It is known at the Boston Massacre, March 5, 1770...the Issue of the Boston newspaper that has carried the sacrifice of Crispus Attucks also had an advertisement of Negroes for sale. Had Americans no sense of the fitness of things? They were 'so eager to abolish their fanciful slavery' to Great Britain, while they were imposing actual slavery on others."[189]

In 1767 the British Parliament passed the Townshend Act which imposed heavy taxations on glass, lead, paint and tea and among other things permitted the general searching of stores, warehouses and even private homes for smuggled goods, which were entering the colonies without tariffs. The colonists in Boston, one of the main slave trading ports in New England, met in a town meeting and declared they would no longer import British goods on which the new taxes had been placed. The Massachusetts colonial legislature sent a letter to the other colonies urging them to support the boycott. King George III and his Cabinet Ministers decided to make an example of the Massachusetts Colony, especially the city of Boston by sending two regiments of British Infantry (about 1,000 foot soldiers) to that city with the aim of striking awe in the inhabitants and frightening the rebels into submission to the royal authority.

After the landing of the troops in Boston Parliament passed the Quartering Act which forced the colonists to provide quarters, fuel, candles and transportation for the British soldiers. By 1770 there were over 3,500 Redcoats patrolling the city. One chilly day on March 5 some young white boys began throwing snowballs at a British sentry. When the Captain of the guard accosted them, a mob of citizens began jeering, taunting and cursing the soldiers, a riot broke up and the tumultuous crowd began throwing stones and threatening the "lobster backs", as they called them, with clubs and sticks. Now keep in mind, these are the same people whose descendants are espousing the watchwords of "law and order" and conservatism today, particularly in regards to the Black man's legitimate quest for "liberty and justice for all." We are told be non-violent and passive in our struggle while at the some being taught to respect Euro-America's violent confrontation with Britain. What a paradox, no wonder so many Black people in this country are so confused and slow to defend themselves against aggression.

In the forefront of this brawl between the Boston citizens and the the British soldiers was a runaway slave named Crispus Attucks who seized the musket from the captain of the guard, punched him in the face and knocked him to the ground. A soldier fired, Attucks caught a bullet in the chest and fell dead. Instantly the crowd was in an uproar and began advancing on the troops, Captain Preston while still lying on the ground gave the order to fire, four whites were killed and many others wounded. The spot on which they fell became hallowed ground to the colonists and from that time until July 4, 1776, March 5 was annually observed as "Crispus Attucks day". In giving his life for this case Brother Crispus Attucks though sincere was misguided. In short as one commentator stated he was a "chump." For at the very same time of his supreme sacrifice most Afrikans in the thirteen colonies, with the full blessings of the law of the land, were in chattel bondage to their white overlords. In fact according to colonial law Attucks status as a runaway slave was in violation. Surely it would have been better for this Brother to have dedicated himself to the service of helping to liberate his own people who were still brutually enslaved by the very same white people who were struggling for their own interest within the framework of the British colonial system. Crispus Attucks died in vain and there are millions of Afrikans in this country and around the world today who can verify that fact.

October 13, 1888 the Massachusetts legislature approved a bill to erect a Crispus Attucks memorial and so it was, exhibiting a statue of a white woman brandishing a colonial flag and a sculpture of an American eagle at her feet. Not a trace of the fact that Crispus Attucks was Black was displayed. Walter Rodney says, ". . .it was no accident that the struggle for American independence started in the leading New England town of Boston."[190] It was the second largest port of the world for the slave trade, New York being the first.

119

THE BOSTON TEA PARTY: AN ACT OF VANDALISM

"...a British West Indian, probably a Jamaican, Samuel Francis, affectionately known as Black Sam...owned the finest hostelry (inn) not only in New York but in colonial America...and it was there the sons of Liberty plotted the dumping of the cases of East India tea into the Hudson."[191]

The colonial boycott against the purchasing of British goods provided smugglers with a heydey of commercial gain which prompted Parliament in 1770 to repeal the Townshend Act except for tax on tea. The home government kept that tax on tea to show that Britain maintained the right to levy taxes on her thirteen colonies in the Americas. The colonists relaxed their boycott which for all practical purposes had been very difficult to keep up because the English and their offspring the Euro-American were literally tea addicts. In spite of the repeal of the tea tax the colonists resolved to drink only the tea that had been smuggled in colonial ports by Dutch merchants. December 16, 1773 three ships of the East India Company owned by British merchants who were given a monopoly of the tea trade in the British colonies tried to land at Boston Harbor. The local legislative body refused the ship's captain permission to dock. That evening about fifty or so white colonists disguised themselves as Mohawk Indians, raided the vessels, beat up the crews and lifted 342 chests of tea from the store rooms and emptied the contents into the sea. Riots in other American colonial ports discouraged further efforts to bring in the company tea.

Note how the colonists planned to blame this act of vandalism on the indigenous Red man. This was a cowardly act indeed, rather than one of heroism as we have been taught through the mis-education of the white man's school system. At least when frustrated Black people rioted in the 1960's they did not try to disguise themselves as anything other than what they were, angry Black folks. Though the destruction of property by these white colonists is held up before us as an act of protest in the colonial American independence movement, yet, the Black man's discontent with unjust treatment as demonstrated in the rebellions of the 1960's and 70's is branded as acts of terrorism and crime in the streets. Thus the ever present and consistent ambiguity of the Euro-American people. Though this particular manifestation of our righteous indignation may not have been the best and wisest way to go. It must be defined by us for what it really was, a protest against injustice and the brutal assassination and harassment of our legitimate Black leadership.

The taxes levied on the tea did not bring in enough revenue to defray the cost of collection and in consequence the tax was repealed.

But the British government decided that something had to be done to assert its authority over the wayward colonists. So Parliament passed the Intolorable Acts in 1774. These new laws ordered the closing of Boston Harbor to commercial trade until the city showed repentance for its "tea party" by paying for the destroyed tea. The colonists having had their disguise exposed refused to pay. To further assert its authority the British sent more troops to Boston under the command of General Gage. When the soldiers arrived outside the city the colonists revolted and rioted in the streets. The businessmen of England supported George III and viewed the impending war between Britain and the thirteen colonies as another avenue of making big profits. Of the eventual American Revolutionary War which grew out of these various local incidents. Durant says, "War...did indeed become a substitute for commerce...great orders for provisions and stores of all kinds...keep up the spirits of the mercantile world, and induce them to consider the American war not so much their calamity as their resource."[192]

Keep in mind here that the main issue was not the tea but the slave trade. John Adams, one of Euro-America's own patriots, says that "Molasses was an essential ingredient in American independence." Rogers writes, "Commerce and politics...were so mixed that rum and liberty were but liquors from the same still. That rum was the spirit of 76 is more than a pun."[193]

AMERICAN SLAVE HOLDERS DECLARE INDEPENDENCE FROM BRITAIN

Thomas Jefferson once said "...that the orangutang preferred Black women to those of his own species." and that Black men "...were void of mental endowment...John Hancock, great patriot, made his fortune as a slave smuggler...Washington...in 1776, sent one of this slaves Tom, by a ship's captain to be exchanged for molasses."[194]

The foregoing historical facts demonstrate the general character and lifestyle of America's founding fathers, the men who convened at the First and Second Continental Congress of the United States and framed their Declaration of Independence. They were slave mongers and brutish tyrants.

British reaction to the Boston civil disturbances of 1774 brought about a police state, town meetings were forbidden; and certain public buildings were taken over for the use of British troops. These circumstances actuated the Virginia colonial assembly to send out a call for a meeting of representatives from the thirteen colonies and Canada to consider joint action against the British. The response of this call resulted in the convening of the First Continential Congress which took place in Philadelphia, Pennsylvania, September 14, 1774. This gathering was essentially a reform movement for most of the delegates in attendance were not disposed to seek independence from Great Britain but rather preferred attempting to effect a reconciliation with the parent government without giving up any colonial rights. This assembly urged the colonies not to carry on any trade with Britain until the Intolerable Acts were repealed. It also denounced many laws passed by Parliament since 1763 and agreed not to import any goods from Britain or Ireland after December 1, 1774 and not to export anything to the British Isles or its West Indian possessions after September 10, 1775 unless the abuses had been corrected.

The First Continental Congress further demanded that the British abandon their efforts to make Massachusetts bow to British authority. The British government now considered the colonists to be in open rebellion and launched a great offensive to crush it. Parliament passed the Restraining Act barring colonists in Massachusetts, Rhode Island and Connecticut from fishing on the Grand Banks of Newfoundland and from trading abroad except with Britain and the British West Indies. The British cabinet then ordered Governor Gage of Massachusetts to arrest all the colonial leaders in that colony, organize a militia and use the troops stationed in Boston to break up the mobs. Gage obeyed the mandates from the home government and ordered troops from Boston to raid Concord and seize the weapons stored by the rebels there.

On the night of April 18, 1775 Paul Revere and William Dawes after drinking freely from the rum distillery at the home of Issac Paul is said to have rode sixteen miles through the night shouting "the British are coming, the British are coming." Actually they staggered quietly through the night to find John Hancock and warn him to flee and escape military arrest and to tell the minuteman of Concord and Lexington to hide their military stores. But Revere was intercepted by the British and thrown in prison. Dawes was unsuccessful because on the morning of April 19th colonial minutemen and Redcoats of the British army clashed into each other at Lexington and the second shot that was "heard around the world" was fired, the first had been lodged in the chest of Crispus Attucks on Boston Commons in 1770. Eight colonists were killed and ten wounded, only one British soldier was wounded. The Minutemen broke camp and the British troops were in hot pursuit.

May 10, 1775 the Second Continental Congress met in Philadelphia to assess the fact that the New England colonies had taken up arms against the king's troop. The delegates were keenly aware of the serious consequences of this action. It was about this time that one of the delegates named Patrick Henry, who himself was a slave owner and had mulatto children by the sexually abused Black women on his Virginia plantation, began sounding the battle cry "I Know not waht path others may take; but as for me, give me liberty, or give me death."[195] The delegates in assembly established the Congress as a central provisional government and adapted the Massachusetts colonial troops who were now engaged in the seige of Boston as their own "Continental Army" and by unaminous vote appointed George Washington as Commander in Chief. On July 2, 1776 the Second Continental Congress declared themselves free of King George III's jurisdiction and two days later ratified and signed their Declaration of Independence.

There were approximately fifty-four dirt farmers and merchants gathered at this convention who had been made economically solvent by the labors of their Black slaves. These wardens of Afrikan captivity met and declared themselves sovereign and independent of Britain. It is said that at the time the United Kingdom's colonial holdings were so vast "the sun never set on the British empire." Most of the signers of America's Declaration of Independence were commercial magnates and land barons. Everyone who signed had to own a large tract of land. If a colonist was employed to work on someone else's land he could not be one of the signers of the Declaration of Independence, in fact, one could not even hold political office in the newly formed government of the United States unless they were a part of the New World aristocracy. The majority of white people who owned land in America at the time had slaves and anyone who had a plantation automatically had slaves for they were essential to the plantation system. Most of the New England representatives, like John Hancock, had been involved in slave smuggling or were in someway connected with the slave trade. Thomas Jefferson who revised the philosophical works of England's John Locke (1632-1704) into the document of America's Declaration of Independence, had children by many of his adolescent female slaves. Jefferson also refused to send these children to school and according to Rogers "At the age of then he had them working all day, and a little above that age in his nail factory. One great horror of the slave-master was to see a Negro with a book. Teaching a slave to read was a crime."[196] This was America at the time of her Declaration of Independence in 1776.

Entertainer Stevie Wonder is somewhat misguided when he states in one of his songs that the signing of this document "set all men free", this is historically incorrect because the thirteen colonies' seccession from the British empire was not an attempt to free the world. And it was never intended that the provisions of the Declaration should apply to Black people at all. Though Dr. King and other civil rights workers have appealed to this document in an effort to make

American practice what she set down on paper and as a tactic of using whatever means that seemed available to them at the time, in many ways it was futile. This is self-evident in the United States governments present rescinding of many of the legal gains and programs that were accorded the race during that period.

BLACK TROOPS USED TO SAVE THE LIVES OF WHITES DURING AMERICA'S REVOLUTIONARY WAR

"After the glowing words of the Declaration of Independence (which didn't apply to Black men), to use slaves and members of a despised race, to fight for the freedom of white men, seemed the last word in contradiction. England was making much of how Negroes had been used so far... Washington saw he must use the Negroes or run the risk of losing the war. He wrote Colonel Henry Lee, December 10, 1775. 'Success will depend on which side can arm the Negro faster.'... Negroes were accepted in such numbers now that General Schuyler wrote, 'Is it consistent with the sons of freedom to trust their all to be defended by slaves?'[197]

Over 5,000 Blacks were among the colonial militia who helped the United States gain its independence from Britain. They fought at all the famous battles which are a part of American folklore, for example at Bunker Hill the British troops were whipping the Americans unmercifully when an Afrikan slave named Peter Salem stepped forth and shot Major John Pitcairn, commander of the British marines, in the chest mortally wounding him. That bullet may have had a lot of the frustration of Salem's personal bondage in it. The fact that he was even permitted to shoot a white man may have in itself been gratifying to this brother. This aggressive initiative on the part of a Black slave saved the day for the American troops.

We are here mentioning the role of Black folks in the American Revolution as a point of historical reference not because we are proud of it but because it actually happened. The questions arises as to why Blacks have fought for their slave masters on this and other occasions. For one such as myself who personally has no regards for whites outside of the general respect due all living creatures it is difficult to comprehend and understand the deep love and affection Blacks used to and many still have for their former slave masters and even their present day exploiters. Yet in my attempts at understanding this remarkable paradox these thoughts come to mind. Although many Black troops who served in America's Revolutionary War did so out of their love and affection for the whites, and seeing no real hope for themselves undertook their master's interest. On the other hand there were those who were probably just trying to make the best from a bad situation. Today, from our vantage point in time rather than just outright condemning these brothers and sisters we should analyse and seek to understand, to the best of our ability, the true meaning of their actions. In our efforts to understand, it does not mean that we should accept, condone or excuse the strange phenomenon that would cause a slave to be so dedicated to his master. But perhaps the answers to this perplexing question will provide us with a key to effectively dealing with Black people of like mind today. Whenever a person, as with the case of the Black slave, is totally separated from everything and everyone that is familiar to him and transplanted into a hostile environment where every decision for his survival is made by another, it brings on a state of mindlessness. If you can imagine what it must have been like for the Afrikan to be captured and brought all the way from his homeland and be held in bondage in a country that was a whole ocean away from his origin and roots, then maybe we can begin to view these events in some kind of logical perspective.

Though we can see nothing to be proud of in these sacrifices made by Afrikans for their white slave masters still history clearly reveals another example of how America would not be in existence today were it not for the Black man. That is why conscious Black people can say unequivocally that legally in accordance with international law as well as morally we owe white folks nothing and they owe us everything. The attitude we must assume at this stage of history is that all things must be viewed in terms of what is in the best interest of the Black race first and in the interest of the world second. This is the way of wisdom, this is the way of a people with self-respect who seek power in the world rather than servitude and subordination to another.

Originally there was opposition to the use of Black troops in the Revolutionary War. On April 28, 1775 George Washington declared that he did not want Blacks to fight for the colonies. Benjamin Franklin, John Hancock and the Council of War of October 8, 1775 opposed the enlistment of Black troops and agreed unanimously to reject all slaves and the majority of Blacks from bearing arms all together. But the founding fathers were later faced with a dilemma which caused them to view this prohibition in a different light. As the war dragged on and on the spirit of patriotism grew weaker and weaker. Many whites seeing no end to the conflict deserted and dropped out of the ranks of the Continental Army, others privately made peace with the British colonial government. This general abandonment of the American revolutionary cause swelled to such a proportion as to cause George Washington to complain of the "lack of patriotism which is infinitely more to be dreaded than the whole forces of Great Britain. From this point on Washington, Jefferson and other American aristocrats were faced with a difficult problem of trying to enlist the common people into the ranks of the fighting forces. This reluctance to participate in the patriotic efforts on the part of the masses was generated by the fact that most of them had no land or landholdings to fight for. For it was clearly understood at this time that this was essentially an economic war rather than a patriotic one. The only ones who seemed to have anything to gain from it were the plantation owners and those who had profitable commercial interest. The leaders of the revolution were trying to get the everyday Euro-American to realize that they had once been prisoners, criminals for Europe was the breeding ground for criminals or serfs, now many of them had a little land and were living better than they could ever have dreamed of in Europe and even though the land barons had most to gain from the war effort there was still enough to go around for everybody, that is everybody but Black folks, for there was virtually nothing for them in America at the time but hard times, bondage and servitude.

Many white slave masters of the south and some of the north did not wish to risk their lives or those of their sons in the fight for liberation so they sent their Black slaves to vicariously take their place in the Continental Army. This fear on the part of whites to face the dangers of death during the Revolutionary War was so widespread that one British officer was moved to observe that there were so many able-bodied, strong and brave Afrikans now enlisted in the American army (there was by this time over 5,000 Blacks in Washington's personal command alone) that it seemed as though Britain was at war with Ethiopa rather than the thirteen colonies of North America. The American army was so lacking in patriotic enlistment that the French government, in possession of Santo Domingo in 1779, sent 800 Black troops to fight for American independence. Among them was Generals Rigaud, Beauvais, Henri Christophe and Martial Besse, some of the future leaders of the Haitian revolution of 1791-1803.

Without a doubt Black troops provided the balance of power that won independence for the United States of America. In fact members of Parliament argued that had it not been for the aid of Black troops, independence would not have been possible for the thirteen colonies at that time. Because of Black troops and the last minute intervention of the French Navy, America won the war with the surrender of General Cornwallis in 1781 and signed a peace treaty with Britain at Paris, September 3, 1873 thus establishing herself as an independent nation. The Black man who served so well in the war effort was compensated for his loyalty by being plunged more deeply into slavery than before the revolutionary war. During the framing of the United States constitutions in 1789 the importation of Afrikan slaves to American shores was permitted for another twenty years and the Black man was counted as three-fifths of a man. In other words it took five Black folks to make up three whole men.[198]

"WHAT TO US IS YOUR FOURTH OF JULY?"

In the year 1852, on the occasion of the celebration of the seventy-sixth anniversary of America's independence from Britain, Frederick Douglass, that great Black abolitionist and orator, was called upon to make a speech, which he did. Following is an exerpt from it.

What, to the American slave, is your Fourth of July? Our answer: a day that reveals to him, more than all other days of the year, the gross injustice and cruelties to which he is the constant victim. To him, your celebration is a sham; your boasted liberty, and unholy license; your national greatness, swelling vanity; your sounds of rejoicing are empty and heartless; your denounciation of tyrants brass fronted impudence; your shouts of liberty and equality, hollow mockery; your prayers and hymns, your sermons and thanksgivings; with all your religious parades and solemnity, are to him, mere bombasts, deceptions, and pious and hypocrisy—a thin veil to cover up crimes which would disgrace a nation of savages. There is not a nation on the earth guilty of practices more shocking and bloody than are the people of the United States at this very hour. Go where you may, search where you will, roam though all the monarchies and depotisims of the Old World, travel through South America, search out every abuse, and when you have found the last, lay your facts side by side of the every day practices of this nation, and you will say with me, that, for revolting barbarity and shameless hypocrisy, American reigns without a rival."[199]

This my beloved Black brothers and sisters, I believe, is a fitting conclusion of the "Fourth of You-Lie". Pamoja Tutashinda —We will win together.

NOTES AND BIBLIOGRAPHY

1. *Sex and Race,* Volume I, J.A. Rogers, Helga M. Rogers, 1270 Fifth Avenue, New York, N.Y. 10029, p. 268.

   Nature Knows No Color Line, J.A. Rogers, Helga M. Rogers, New York, N.Y. 10029, p.55.

2. *The Seventh-day Adventist Bible Commentary,* Volume I, Review and Herald Publishing Association, Washington, D. C., pp. 84-88.

   World's Great Men of Color, Volume I, J.A. Rogers, Helga M. Rogers, New York, N.Y. 10029, p. xiii.

3. *Sex and Race,* Volume I, J.A. Rogers, Helga M. Rogers, New York, N.Y. 10029, p. 28.

4. *Ibid.,* p. 25.

   God, The Bible and The Man's Destiny — I. Barashango, Fourth Dynasty Publishing Co., 3415 18th Street, N.E. 20008, pp. 23-24.

   Authorized Version of the Holy Bible, Genesis Chapters 1 and 2.

5. *Sex and Race,* Volume I, J.A. Rogers, Helga M. Rogers, New York, N.Y. 10029, p. 28.

6. Ibid., p. 32.

7. *Washington Star* Article, May 5, 1979.

   Black Man of the Nile, Yosef ben-Jochannon, Alkebulan Books, 40 West 135th Street, N.Y.C., N.Y. 10037, 1970, p. 6c.

   New Standard Encyclopedia, Volume A—Standard Education Society, Inc., Chicago, Ill. 1961, p. A-69.

8. *Natures Knows No Color Line,* J.A. Rogers, Helga M. Rogers, New York, N.Y. 10029, 1952, pp. 33-34, 23.

9. *100 Amazing Fact About The Negro,* J.A. Rogers, Helga M. Rogers, New York, N.Y. 10029, 1957, p. 9.

   Anacalypsis, Volume I, G. Higgins, London, 1836, New York 1927, p. 286.

10. *Authorized Version of the Holy Bible,* Ezekiel 1:26-28; Daniel 7:9.

    God, The Bible and The Black Man's Destiny—I. Barashango, IVth Dynasty Publishing Co., Washington, D. C. 20018, 1982, pp. 2, 7.

11. *Sex and Race,* Volume I, J.A. Rogers, Helga M. Rogers, New York, N.Y. 10029, 1967, p. 196.

    They Came Before Columbus — I. Van Sertina, Random House, New York, 1976, pp. 29-30.

    Man, God and Civilization, J.G. Jackson, University Books, Inc., New Hyde Park, N.Y, 1972, p. 28.

12. *The Afrikan Origin of Civilization,* A. Diop, Lawrence Hill and Company, New York, Westport, 1974, p. 298.

    Sex and Race, Volume I, J.A. Togers, New York, N.Y. 10029, p. 196.

    Black Man of the Nile, Yosef ben Jochannon, Alkebulan Books, N.Y.C., N.Y. 10037, 1970, p. 52.

13. *100 Amazing Facts About The Negro,* J.A. Rogers, Helga M. Rogers, New York, N.Y. 10029, 1970, p. 30.

14. *Sex and Race,* Volume I, J.A. Rogers, Helga M. Rogers, New York, N.Y. 10029, pp. 32, 28.

15. *Colliers Encyclopedia,* Volume 21, p. 384.

16. *Ethiopia and the Missing Link in African History,* S.M. Means, D. Hakim, 842 M.L.K. Jr Dr. S.W., Atlanta, Georgia 30314, 1980, p. 81.

    The Afrikan Origin of Civilization, C.A. Diop, Lawrence Hill & Company, New York, Westport, 1974, p. 270.

17. *Sex and Race,* Volume I, J.A. Rogers, Helga M. Rogers, N.Y.C. 10029, p. 196.

    Ethiopia and the Missing Link in African History, S.M. Means, D. Hakim, Atlanta, Georgia 30314, 1980, p. 88.

18. *Encyclopedia Americana,* Volume 14, p. 689; Volume 16, p. 726.

19. *Sex and Race,* Volume I, J.A. Rogers, Helga M. Rogers, N.Y.C. 10029, p. 197.

20. *Ibid.,* p. 197.

    Stolen Legacy, George G.M. James, Julian Richardson Associates, 540 McAllister Street, San Francisco, Calif., 1976, Chapter III.

21. *All Color Book of Roman Mythology,* P. Croft, Octopus Books Limited, 59 Grosvenor Street, London WI, 1974, p. 50.

22. *New Encyclopedia Britannica,* Volume 3, p. 597.

23. *Sex and Race,* Volume I, J.A. Rogers, Helga M. Rogers, N.Y.C. 10029, p. 196, 197.

24. *Anacalypsis,* Volume I, G. Higgins, University Books, Inc., New Hyde Park, N.Y., p. 59.

25. *World Book Encyclopedia,* Volume I, pp. 808-809.

26. *The Story of Patriarchs and Prophets,* E.G. White, Review and Herald Publishing Association, Washington, D.C. 1958, p. 87.

27. *Black Man of the Nile,* Yosef ben-Jochannon (See above), pp. 46-47.

    They All Look Alike! All?!, Yosef ben-Jochannon (See above), p. 16.

28. *Ethiopia the Missing Link in African History,* S.M. Means, (See above), pp. 15-28.

29. *Authorized Version of the Holy Bible,* Genesis Chapters 3 and 4.

30. *Our Oriental Heritage,* W. Durant, Simon and Schuster, 650 Fifth Avenue, New York, N.Y. 10020, 1963, p. 330.

A Commentary on the Holy Bible, J.R. Dummelow, The MacMillan Company, N.Y.C., 1947, pp. 6, 7, 9.

Harpers Bible Dictionary, M.S. and J.L. Miller, Harper & Row Publishers, 49 East 33rd Street, N.Y.C., 10016, 1961, pp. 148-149, 780.

God, The Bible and The Black Man's Destiny—I. Barashango, (See above), p. 30.

31. *World Book Encyclopedia*, Volume I, pp. 6-7.

32. *They All Look Alike! All?!*, Yosef ben-Jochannon, (See above), p. 16.

33. *Black Man of the Nile*, Yosef ben-Jochannon, (See above), 1970, p. 64.

34. *The African Origin of Civilization*, C.A. Diop, (See above), p. 68.

35. *Sex and Race*, Volume I, J.A. Rogers, (See above), pp. 29, 30.

   The Black Mentally Retarded Offender, A.R. Harvey and T.L. Carr, United Church of Christ, Commission for Racial Justice, 105 Madison Avenue, N.Y.C. 10016, 1982, pp. 178-81.

36. *The Cultural Unity of Black Africa*, C.A. Diop, Third World Press, 7524 Cottage Grove Avenue, Chicago, Illinois 60619, 1978, p. 9.

37. *Ibid.*, for a thorough discussion of this indeliable diversity read the entire publication cited above.

38. *Nature Knows No Color Line*, J.A. Rogers, (See above), p. 31.

39. *The Chness Theory of Color Confrontation*, Frances Chness Welsing. Read the entire work.

40. *Black Books Bulletin*, Volume 5, No. 4, Third World Press, 7524 Cottage Grove Avenue, Chicago, Illinois 60619, p. 31.

41. *The Cultural of Black Afrika*, C.A. Diop, (See above), p. 87.

42. *Encyclopedia Britannica*, Volume 8, 1939, p. 845.

43. *The Cultural Unity of Black Africa*, C.A. Diop, (See above), p. 180.

44. Chness Theory of Color Confrontation, Francis Chness Welsing, p. 8.

45. *Heard the Call Ya'll*, a recording by Minister Louis Farrakhan, Final Call Inc., P.O. Box 8154, Chicago, Il. 60680.

46. *The Cultural Unity of Black Afria*, C.A. Diop, (See above), p. 71.

47. *Ibid.*, pp. 176-177; 29.

48. *Ibid.*, p. 132.

49. *Nature Knows No Color Line*, J.A. Rogers, (See above), p. 28.

   The Jesus Scroll, Donovan Joyce, The New American Library, Inc., 1301 Avenue of the Americas, New York, N.Y. 10019, 1974, pp. 76-77.

50. *The Cultural Unity of B ack Africa*, C.A. Diop, (See above), p. 133.

51. *Ibid.*, p. 127.

52. *Ibid.*, p. 128.

53. *Herodotus The Histories*, Penguin Books Inc., 7110 Ambassador Road, Baltimore, Maryland 21207, 1971, pp. 56-57.

From "Superman" To Man, J.A. Rogers, (See above), pp. 82-83.

54. *Herodotus The Histories*, Penquin Books Inc., (See above), p. 276.

55. *the Cultural Unity of Black Africa*, C.A. Diop, (See above), pp. 127-128.

Authorized Version of the Holy Bible, Genesis Chapter 30:1-24.

56. *Foundations of the Black Nation*, I.A. Obadele I, Julian Richardson Associates, 540 McAllister Street, San Francisco, California 94102, 1975, pp. 42-48.

57. *The Cultural Unity of Black Africa*, C.A. Diop, (See above), p. 230.

58. *Herodotus The Histories*, (See above), p. 163.

59. *The Cultural Unity of Black Africa*, C.A. Diop, (See above), p. 63.

60. *Herodotus The Histories*, (See above), p. 243.

61. *Ibid.*, pp. 244-245.

62. *The Afrikan Origin of Civilization*, C.A. Diop, (See above), p. 4.

63. *Herodotus The Histories*, (See above), pp. 199, 56-57.

64. *From "Superman" To Man*, J.A. Rogers, (See above), pp. 82-83.

65. *Sex and Race*, Volume III, J.A. Rogers (See above), p. 287.

Sex and Race, Volume II, J.A. Rogers (See above), p. 398.

66. *From Babylon to Timbukto*, R.R. Windsor, Exposition Press, Inc. 50 Jericho Turnpike, Jericho, New York 11753, 1969, pp. 19-20.

67. *Herodotus The Histories*, (See above), p. 257.

68. *Ibid.*, p. 266.

World Book Encyclopedia, Vol. H, p. 176.

69. *Herodotus The Histories*, (See above), p. 266.

70. *From "Superman" To Man*, J.A. Rogers, (See above), p. 45.

71. *Herodotus The Histories*, (See above), p. 262.

72. *Ibid.*, p. 242.

73. *Ibid.*, pp. 262-263.

74. *Ibid.*, p. 261.

75. *Sex and Race*, Volume I, J.A. Rogers, (See above), p. 197.

76. *Stolen Legacy*, George G.M. James, (See above), p. 10.

77. *The Afrikan Origin of Civilization*, C.A. Diop, (See above), p. 251.

78. *Ibid.*, p. 113.

79. *Man, God, and Civilization*, C.A. Diop, (See above), p. 251.

80. *Stolen Legacy*, George G.M. James, (See above), pp. 41-53; 176, 178.

81. *Nature Knows No Color Line*, J.A. Rogers (See above), p. 31.

82. *All Color Book of Roman Mythology*, P. Croft (See above), pp. 22-23.

   Imperial Rome, M. Hadas, Time Incorporated, New York, 1965, p. 10.

83. *Man, God, and Civilization*, J.G. Jackson, (See above), pp. 252-253.

84. *The African Origin of Civilization*, C.A. Diop, (See above), pp. 118-119.

85. *Sex and Race*, Volume I, J.A. Rogers, (See above), p. 151.

86. *Sex and Race*, Volume III, J.A. Rogers, (See above), p. ix.

87. *Sex and Race*, Volume I, J.A. Rogers, (See above), p. 151.

   The African Origin of Civilization, C.A. Diop, (See above), p. 119.

   African Origins of the Major "Western Religions", Yosef ben-Jochannon, (See above), 1970, p. 75.

88. *The African Origin of Civilization*, C.A. Diop, (See above), p. 143.

89. *The Cultural Unity of Black Africa*, C.A. Diop, (See above), p. 57.

90. *Nature Knows No Color Line*, J.A. Rogers, (See above), pp. 234-242.

91. *Ibid.*, pp. 275-289.

   Ethiopia and the Missing Link in African History, S.M. Means, (See above), p. 126.

92. *Sex and Race*, Volume III, J.A. Rogers, (See above), pp. 3: 251.

93. *Anacalysis*, Volume II, G. Higgins, (See above), p. 305.

94. *Sex In History*, R. Tannahill, Stein and Day Publishers, Scarborough House, Barcliff Manor, N.Y. 10510, 1980, pp. 125-126.

95. *African History*, E. Sweeting and L. Edmond, African American International Press, P.O. Box 775, Flushing, New York 11352, 1973, p. 23.

96. *Encyclopedia Britannica*, Volume 20, 1939, p. 396.

97. *African History*, E. Sweeting and L. Edmond, (See above) p. 23.

98. *Ethiopia and the Missing Link in African History*, S.M. Means, (See above), p. 160.

   Profiles in African Heritage, E.L. Jones, Frayn Printing Co., 2518 Western Avenue, Seattle, Washington 98121, 1972. pp. 45;125.

   Imperial Rome, M. Hadas, Time Incorporated, New York, 1965, p. 10.

99. *Encyclopedia Britannica*, Volume 20, 1939, p. 397.

100. *Profiles in African Heritage*, E.L. Jones, (See above), p. 127.

101. *Man, God, and Civilization*, J.G. Jackson, (See above), p. 261.

102. *Ibid.*, p. 266.

103. *Nature Knows No Color Line*, J.A. Rogers, (See above), p. 69.

104. *Caesar and Christ*, W. Durant, Simon and Schuster, Inc., 630 Fifth

Avenue, New York, N.Y. 10020, 1944, p. 478.

105. *Ibid.*, p. 478.

106. *From "Superman" To Man*, J.A. Rogers, (See above), p. 46.

107. *The Destruction of Black Civilization*, C. Williams, Third World Press, (See above), 1974.

108. *African Origins of the Major "Western Religions"*, Yosef ben-Jochannon, (See bove), p. 75.

109. *Nature Knows No Color Line*, J.A. Rogers, (See above), p. 40.

Sex and Race, Volume I , J.A. Rogers, (See above), pp. 265; 81, 292. There is an abundance of evidence supporting this fact which will be discussed in the forthcoming series. *Black Historical Facts on the Life of Jesus*, by I. Barashango. IVth Dynasty Publishing Co.

110. *Stolen Legacy*, George G.M. James, (See above), p. 154.

African Origins of tho Major "Western Religions", Yosef ben-Jochannon, (See above), p. 75 and the whole of Chapter Two.

111. *The Age of Faith*, W. Durant, Simon and Schuster, Inc., 650 Fifth Avenue, New York, N.Y. 10020, 1950, p. 519.

112. *Crimes of Christianity*, G.W. Foote and J.M. Wheeler, pp. 6-7, 29, 31, 32.

113. *World's Great Men of Color*, J.A. Rogers, (See above), p. 119.

114. *Funk and Wagnalls Standard Reference Encyclopedia*, Volume 24, 1943, p. 3289.

World Book Encyclopedia, Volume E, 1965, p. 320(0)

115. *The Cultural Unity of Black Africa*, C.A. Diop, (See above), p. 133.

116. *Worlds Great Men of Color*, J.A. Rogers, (See above), p. 119.

117. *Sex and Race*, Volume I, J.A. Rogers, (See above), p. 198.

118. *Anacalypsis*, Volume I, E. Higgins, p. 153, Volume II, pp. 1-4. (See above)

119. *The Chness Theory of Color Confrontation*, Frances Chness Welsing.

120. *Our Oriental Heritage*, W. Durant, (See above), p. 217.

121. *Anacalypsis*, Volume II, G. Higgins (See above), pp. 175-176.

122. *Washington Post Parade Magazine*, May 30, 1982, p. 16.

123. *Sex and Race*, Volume I, J.A. Rogers, (See above), pp. 197, 198.

124. *Recreation of the Gods*, A Record Album by Rufus Harley (Jazz Bagpipes).

125. *Funk & Wagnalls Standard Reference Encyclopedia*, Volume 9, 1967, p. 3289.

Ibid., Volume 9, p. 3291.

126. *New Standard Encyclopedia,* Standard Education Society, Inc., Chicago, Ill. 1960, Volume F, p. 47.

127. *Ibid.,* Volume F, p. 51.

128. *Ibid.,* Volume C, p. 146.

129. Henry II and his ambitious and notorious wife Eleanor of Aquitaine are the subjects of a somewhat historical accurate motion picture "The Lion In Winter". Though it is not the intent of this book to recommend movies, nevertheless we found this particular one, as a result of the producers quest for realism, to be historically true to life in its portrayal of the squalor and general under-development of the English monarchy, nobility and the common people of that period.

130. *The Black Messiah,* A.B. Cleage, Sheed and Ward, N.Y.C., 1968, pp. 37-38.

131. *Man, God and Civilization,* J.G. Jackson, (See above), pp. 261-262.

132. *The Age of Faith,* W. Durant, (See above), p. 835.

The Destruction of Black Civilization, C. Williams, (See above), pp. 171—186.

135. *The Reformation,* W. Durant, Simon and Schuster, New York: 1957, pp. 37-43.

136. *The Age of Faith,* W. Durant, (See above), p. 680.

137. The Last Poets speaking on European Masons only able to attain 33 degrees without falling apart.

138. *Africa: Mother of Western Civilization,* Yosef ben-Jochannon.

They All Look Alike! All?!, Yosef ben-Jochanon.

139. *Man, God and Civilization,* J.G. Jackson, (See above), p. 273.

140. *The Reformation,* W. Durant, (See above), p. 65.

141. *Ibid.,* p. 113.

142. *Ibid.,* p. 532.

143. *Sex and Race,* Volume I, J.A. Rogers, (See above), p. 198.

144. *Nature Knows No Color Line,* J.A. Rogers, (See above), pp. 76, 78, 83-86, 88-91.

145. *The age of Reason Begins,* W. Durant and A. Durant, Simon and Schuster, New York: 1861, p. 9.

146. *Ibid.,* p. 12.

147. *Ibid.,* p. 53.

148. *Ibid.,* p. 131, 136, 137.

149. *Ibid.,* p. 152.

150. *The Age of Faith*, W. Durant (See above), pp. 821-822.

151. *Philosophy and Opinions of Marcus Garvey*, A.J. Garvey, Julian Richardson Associates, (See above), 1967, pp. 37-38.

152. *The World and Africa*, W.E.B. DuBois, International Publishers co., Inc., N.Y.C., 1969, pp. 60-61.

153. *Authorized Verson of the Holy Bible*, Proverbs 29:2.

154. *Capitalism & Slavery*, E. Williams, University of North Carolina Press, 1966, p. 108.

155. *From Slavery to Freedom*, John Hope Franklin, Vintage Books A Division of Random House, New York, 1969, p. 67.

156. *Capitolism and Slavery*, E. Williams (See above), p. 108.

157. *How Europe Underdeveloped Africa*, Walter Rodney, Howard University Press, Washington, D. C. 1974, -. 84.

158. *Ibid.*, p. 85.

159. *Capitolism and Slavery*, E. Williams, (See above), p. 108.

160. *From Slavery to Freedom: A History of Negro Americans*, John Hope Franklin, (See above), p. 160.

161. *The Black Jacobins*, C.L. R. James, Vintage Books, A Division of Random House, New York, 1963, pp. 6-26.

162. *Washington Post Parade Magazine*, Significa June 20, 1982.

163. *Black Folk: Then and Now*, W.E.B. DuBois, p. 152.

164. *No More Lies the Myth and the Reality of American History*, R.C. Gregory, Harper & Row Publishers, Inc., 10 East 53rd Street, New York, N.Y. 10022, 1972, pp. 96-97.

Afrikan People and European Holidays, Book I, (See title page of this book), pp. 25, 45.

165. *West Indian Nations: A New History*, P.M. Sherlock, p. 60.

166. *From Columbus to Castro*, Eric Eilliams, p. 88.

167. *Rousseau and Revolution*, W. Durant, Simon and Schuster, New York, 1967, p. 63.

168. *Washington Post Parade Magazine*, Significa, May 9, 1982.

169. *Africa Gifts to America*, J.A. Rogers, (See above), p. 76.

170. *The World and Africa*, W.E.B. DuBois, (See above), p. 54.

171. *The British In The Caribbean*, Cyril Hamshere, p. 143.

172. *The World and Africa*, W.E.B. DuBois, (See above), pp. 60-61.

173. *Pioneer For Black Freedom in the New World: Cudjoe of Jamaica*, Milton G. McFarlane, p. 7.

174. *The British in the Caribbean,* Cyril Hamshere, p. 140.

175. *Pioneer For Black Freedom in the New World: Cudjoe of Jamaica,* Milton C. McFarlane, p. 8.

176. *The British in the Caribbean,* Cyril Hamshere, p. 142.

177. *Maroon Societies,* Richard Price, p. 22.

178. *Foundations of the Black Nation,* I.A. Obadele I, New African Creed No. 4, p. 152.

179. *West Indian Nations: A New History,* P.M. Sherlock, pp. 204-205.

180. *Ibid.,* p. 202.

181. *Africa's Gift to America,* J.A. Rogers, (See above), p. 42.

182. *Ibid.,* p. 42.

183. *Ibid.,* pp. 39-40.

184. *Capitolism & Slavery,* Eric Williams, (See above), p. 124.

185. *Africa's Gift to America,* J.A.Rogers, (See above), pp. 40, 44, 42.

186. *Afrikan People and European Holidays: A Mental Genocide,* Book I, pp. 18-23.

    Africa's Gift to America, J.A. Rogers, (See above), p. 44.

187. *Ibid.,* p. 37.

188. *Foundations of the Black Nation,* I.A. Obadele I, p. 152, New Afrikan Creed No. 5 and No. 6.

189. *Africa's Gift to America,* J.A. Rogers, (See above), pp. 98, 103.

190. *How Europe Underdeveloped Africa,* Walter Rodney (See above), p. 87.

191. *Africa's Gift to America,* J.A. Rogers, (See above), p. 113.

192. *Rousseau and Revolution,* W. Durant and A. Durant (See above), p. 711.

193. *Africa's Gift to America,* J.A. Rogers (See above), pp. 43.

194. *Sex and Race III,* J.A. Rogers, (See above), p. 250.

    Africa's Gift to America, J.A. Rogers (See above), pp. 81, 44, 35.

195. *100 Amazing Facts About the Negro,* J.A. Rogers, (See above), pp. 8, 29.

196. *Africa's Gift to America,* J.A. Rogers (See above), p. 220.

197. *Ibid.,* pp. 103, 106, 108.

198. *Eye Witness The Negro in American History,* W.L. Katz, Pitman Publishing Corporation, New York-Toronto-London, 1968, p. 50.

    The Negro Almanac, H.A. Ploski and R.C. Brown, Jr., Bellwether Publishing Company, Inc., 167 East 67th Street, New York 10021, 1967, pp. 64, 68.

199. *Selections From the Writing of Frederick Douglass,* International Publishing Co., Inc., New York, 1945, pp. 52-53.

✳ MAIL ORDER FORM ✳

When ordering audio tapes list how many of each selection You
desire in the corresponding numbered box.

1. *The Real Jesus Was A Black Man* ----------------------------------
2. *The Marital Life Of Jesus And His Son Barabbas* ----------------
3. *Black Historical Facts On The LIfe Of Jesus*
   Volume I ---
4. *Black Historical Facts On The Life Of Jesus*
   Volume II --
5. *Amazing Black Facts Of The Bible: An Historical*
   Outline ---
6. *Afrikan Origin Of The Christian Church* ----------------------------
7. *Black Woman Queen Mother Of The Universe* ------------------
8. *Afrikan Origin Of The Human Species* -------------------------------
9. *In The Beginning Was The Black Race* --------------------------------
10. *Portrait Of The Eternal People* --------------------------------------
11. *The Gospel According To Ol' Nat The Prophet* --------------------
12. *And The Word Of The Lord Came By Marcus Garvey* -----------
13. *A Black Revolutionary Called Jesus* --------------------------------
14. *Afrikan Warriors In The Bible* --
15. *How To Find Black History In The Bible* ---------------------------
16. *Resurrecting The Hidden Cosmic Powers*
    Of The Afrikn Mind --
17. *The Bible: Word Of God Or Work Of Man* --------------------------
18. *It's Madness! Black People And Whitefolks Holidays:*
Dr. Barashango In Concert From A Hip Hop Perspective ----------
19. *Great Black Women In The Bible Pt. 1* ----------------------------
20. *Great Black Women Of The Bible Pt. 2* ----------------------------
21. *The Historical Reality: Christopher Columbus DID*
    NOT Discover America ---
22. *Afrikan People And European Holidays:A Mental*
    Genocide, The Tape (Misgivivg Day) -------------------------------
23. *Afrikan People And European Holidays:A Mental*
    Genocide, The Tape (Xmas) --
24. *Kwanzaa In The Bible* --

❧   **PLEASE TURN PAGE FOR MAILING INSTRUCTIONS**   ❦

ALL THE AUDIO TITLES LISTED ABOVE
ARE FULL 90 MINUTE TAPES ❧ ❦ *$12.00 Each*

Afrikan People and European Holidays vol 1	$12.95
Afrikan People and European Holidays vol 2	$14.95
Afrikan Woman the Original Guardian Angel	$14.95
Afrikan Genesis: Amazing Stories of Man's Beginnings	$18.00
God, the Bible and the Black Man's Destiny	$19.95

❧❧❧❧❧❧❧❧❧❧❧❧❧❧❧❧❧❧❧❧❧❧❧❧❧❧❧

Please include $2.00 per item for shipping and handling

Name_____

Address_____

City/State_____**Zip**_____

Total Amount Enclosed*_____

Remit to: AFRIKAN WORLD BOOKS
POB 16447
Baltimore, MD 21217
410-383-2006
afrikanworldword@aol.com